Take the Fear Out of Franchising

Dr. John P. Hayes

Praise for Take the Fear Out of Franchising

"I've been an avid fan of John's for years, following his work, experiencing his passion for growing small companies into larger ones and discovering why, when the franchise model became so legendary, that John's integrity added volumes to its profound contribution to the economic growth of our country. This book is a must for any prospective franchisee or franchisor, as it provides a reliable methodology and practice for succeeding where many fear to fail. Thanks, John. A great book."

Michael E. Gerber
Author of The New York Times
#1 Most Successful E-Myth Books,
and, according to INC Magazine,
"The World's #1 Small Business Guru Worldwide!"

"Too few CEOs really fully understand the value of turning a great brand into a great franchise. John has been an operating member of CEOClubs.org and has been an outstanding academic teaching the subject. Rather than fear franchising, just read this book."

Joe Mancuso, Founder
CEO CLUBS International, Inc.

"*Take the Fear Out of Franchising* is truly a must read for anyone considering the purchase of a franchise. It's a step-by-step, realistic guide on how to make one of the most important decisions of your life. After almost 30 years in franchising, I have not come across a more direct and useful book about franchising."

Tony Foley, Vice President of Global Sales
United Franchise Group

"As the Chairman of Ascendant Global, the worldwide division of Ascendant Group in the U.S., specializing in CEO Branding, and the CEO of Vantage Business Development Solutions in Egypt & the Middle East, I'm constantly meeting with CEOs who are either struggling with international franchises or suffering from the franchise FEAR syndrome that you have so comprehensively dissected in your book. I believe that your book will encourage many of the CEOs in the Region (Middle East & Northern Africa) to make quicker more informed decisions regarding buying into the franchise world in a more professional manner."

Ezz Eldin El Nattar
Chief Executive Officer
Vantage BDS

"I've been in the franchise industry for over 25 years, most of that time producing franchise events throughout the U.S. and around the world. As a result, I've come to know thousands of executives in every sector of the franchise industry.

"John Hayes' understanding of all aspects of the franchise industry is truly unique. This understanding comes from being a franchisee, franchisor, speaker, teacher, PR specialist, and writer. His latest book illustrates the amazing ability John has when it comes to breaking down complex issues and explaining them in a simple, easy to comprehend way. This is an important book to read if you're going to buy a franchise!"

Tom Portesy, President
MFV Expositions

"Before you look at any franchise investment you'll want Dr. John Hayes's franchising wisdom. Use this book as your serious guide in choosing a franchise. It's the road less traveled for savvy franchise buyers."

Joe Caruso
Principal
Franchise Development & Recruitment
Franchise-Info.ca

"Would you pay $10 before you spent $10,000? Every day of the year if it would give me the answers to success in franchising. This book by Dr. John Hayes has those answers!"

John L. Barry, CEO
Franchise Sales International

"*Take The Fear Out of Franchising* is an outstanding resource which helps you make the right franchising decision and steps to protect yourself from a franchising nightmare. John Hayes delivers real life experience in franchising, and he teaches key franchising tenets to take the fear of franchising away."

Khalid Al-Zanki
Founder & CEO, Alzanki Enterprises

"A great read for anyone who is thinking about opening up their own business or thinking about becoming a franchisee. You did an outstanding job putting the facts out there. Great book."

Robert E. Tunmire
Executive Vice President
The Dwyer Group

"Fear is often the #1 reason why people end up not moving forward in buying a franchise. It is often not the money (they have it); it may not even be the lack of spouse's support (they've got that support). Rather, it's the fear of failure, it's the fear of the unknown, it's the fear that they may not make it. Ultimately it's an emotional reason driven by fear that keeps them from going forward in buying the franchise…I see it all the time. This book, by franchise veteran Dr. John Hayes, will help you address that fear. Dr. Hayes is a master at getting past all the hype and taking an honest look at buying a franchise."

Jason Killough,
Certified Franchise Executive and Developer
The Entrepreneur Authority

"Franchising is a brilliant business model, but it's not for everyone. Over the years, John Hayes has guided thousands of people on their journey to explore franchising. His book hits the mark on deciding if a franchise is right for you and, if so, what you need to know before signing that dotted line.

"The tenets are simple but often overlooked, and John's advice is invaluable. This is a must-read for anyone who's considering entering the world of franchising."

David Mattson
CEO, Sandler Training

"My prediction: Literary critics and book reviewers will enthusiastically commend, hail, and applaud your latest writing, so that Taking the Fear Out of Franchising will accelerate to the top-ten list of books."

Tom Feltenstein
Power Marketing Academy

OTHER BEST-SELLING BOOKS
BY DR. JOHN P. HAYES

7 Dirty Little Secrets of Franchising:
Protect Your Franchise Investment

Buy "Hot" Franchises Without Getting Burned

101 Questions to Ask Before You Invest in a Franchise

12 Amazing Franchise Opportunities for 2015

Start Small Finish Big
Fifteen Key Lessons to Start and Run
Your Own Successful Business
with Fred DeLuca, co-founder of Subway

Franchising: The Inside Story
with John Kinch

You Can't Teach a Kid to Ride a Bike at a Seminar
with David Sandler

Visit:
BooksByJohnHayes.com

E-Book Publication Date: 2017

Paperback Publication Date: 2017

ISBN: 978-0-9975536-3-5

Publisher: BizComPress

First edition published 2017

BizComPress

A division of BizCom Associates

BizComPress.com

1400 Preston Rd. #305, Plano, TX 75093

Read this Disclaimer

Take the
Fear
Out of
Franchising

Dr. John P. Hayes

CONTENTS

Foreword xv

Part I
A Simple Concept That Works for Many, But Not All 1

Part II
Know Thyself Because the Franchisor Might Not 13

Part III
Commit to These Franchise Tenets, If You Can 31

Part IV
Can You Accept the Risk of Starting a Business? 47

Part V
Pay Attention to the Only Data That Matters 61

Afterword 81

17 Steps to Successfully
Buying a Franchise 85

Funding Your Franchise Acquisition:
Where Do You Get the Money? 99

Foreign Investors:
Use Franchising To Get
A U.S. Green Card 107

Franchise Terms and Resources 111

Franchise Resources 117

Author's Biography 121

FOREWORD

For more than 25 years, I've taught *The A to Zs of Buying a Franchise* at expositions and conferences worldwide, and on every occasion I've asked this same question:

Why don't you already own a franchise?

My seminars usually include 100 to 300 people at a time, and the answers to my question vary from "I don't have enough information" to "I don't know which one to buy" to "I can't figure out how much I can earn if I own a franchise."

Fair enough. But the one thing all of the answers have in common is an unstated four-letter word that means *False Evidence Appearing Real*: FEAR!

Of course, not many people want to admit they're afraid to buy a business, especially when they're sitting among a roomful of strangers talking to a seminar leader whom they've just met. So the "F" word doesn't get mentioned, but it's always present, and it's constantly gnawing away creating doubt in the minds of prospective franchisees.

And to that I say: Hooray!

Because you should be fearful of franchising.

Are you a franchise misfit?

If you search the word "franchise" on the web, or you read

popular periodicals that cover the broad topic of franchising, it's easy to find negative information that is intended to either make you fearful of franchising or persuade you not to buy a franchise.

Much of that information is nonsense, and it often comes from failed franchisees who may feel better by getting even with a franchisor or with franchising in general. But the truth of the matter is that most of these people failed because they were franchise misfits. They are good people who never should have been sold a franchise.

And that's one of the reasons why you need to be fearful of franchising. If you show interest in buying a franchise, and you've got the money to invest, or you can borrow the money, there are many, many franchise companies that will *help* you buy a franchise, even by loaning you money. Franchise sales-people — most of whom are hard-working, honest people — earn their livelihoods via commissions from franchise sales. They're not looking for reasons to deny selling a franchise, especially to someone who shows interest.

However, most people should not buy franchises. Even though franchising is a very simple concept, which I explain thoroughly in this book, it's not a concept that works for everyone. And yet, franchise sales people tend to believe that their job is not to judge but to sell. "I don't know who will or won't succeed in our franchise," I've been told many times by franchise sales representatives. "My job is to present the opportunity. The buyer should make sure this is the right business for them."

Indeed! If you are going to buy a franchise it *is* your responsibility to make certain not only that a particular business is right for you but that franchising makes sense for you, too.

Franchising may not be for you

And I maintain that if you're a good fit for franchising there's no safer way to get into business for yourself and to begin building personal wealth than to buy a franchise. However, evidenced by the abundance of franchise horror stories, franchising is not for everyone.

I don't for a moment think that all the people who share their franchise horror stories make them up. They may exaggerate parts of the story, and they may totally shirk any responsibility for the negative outcome of the story, but the stories are essentially true. Countless people have lost their life savings and some have been forced into bankruptcy after buying franchises. Loved ones have even claimed that family members took their own lives after suffering the indignity of failure in a franchise. These are extremely sad and unfortunate stories to hear.

But for the most part, they are also avoidable stories. Failed franchisees often fight back when they hear those words because they claim they were cheated or defrauded by a franchisor or by a franchisor's representative. I'll quickly add that their explanation is possible.

Franchisors are not created equally. Some are better than others. Some are more experienced than others. Some are more honest than others. Some may purposely use franchising to access other people's money and talent to create their own financial fortunes. But I've spent nearly 40 years in franchising and it seems to me that most franchisors have the best of intentions and they want their franchisees to succeed.

My experience includes owning multiple franchises through the years, including one that placed and serviced ATM machines and another that bought and sold real estate. I know that franchisors must divulge pertinent information about their businesses prior to awarding a franchise to a buyer, and that's why I'm confident that most of the franchise horror stories are exaggerated. They're intended to discredit franchisors and franchising in general.

Nonetheless, the horror stories are scary. They create fear of franchising, and rightfully so.

You can avoid the horror stories

But let me assure you that almost anyone who can read can avoid personally experiencing a franchise horror story.

In the United States, the government has made certain that franchisors must expose their blemishes, including failures and disputes with franchisees, while attempting to sell franchises. Even outside the U.S., where franchise regulations do not exist or minimally exist, a reasonably intelligent person can "get the goods" on a franchise business or a franchisor and use that information to make an informed decision about the value of a franchise opportunity.

To help you make an informed decision, I've written *Take the Fear Out of Franchising*. This book shows you how to protect yourself from a franchise horror story. Early in the book, I teach you about five franchise tenets that quickly help you understand why franchising works, and why it will or won't work for you.

Then, with the help of two franchise attorneys, I show you how to investigate franchise opportunities. I also include my unique perspective about investigating franchising as an industry. I say it's mostly a waste of your time – it will do more to create fear than anything else. I think you'll appreciate my approach, and you'll be able to use it to investigate franchise opportunities that make sense for you. That is, of course, providing that franchising makes sense for you.

Many people use franchising as a means to business success and personal wealth. You can, too, if you'll verify that you're a good fit for franchising, and if you'll commit to the five franchise tenets that I discuss in this book.

- Dr. John P. Hayes

PART I
A Simple Concept That Works for Many, But Not All

The first time I really thought about franchising was in the spring of 1979 while I was a young college professor at Temple University in Philadelphia where I was the head of the magazine writing sequence.

A man who described himself as a "franchisor" called to ask if I could write an operations manual for his business. I said I could even though while he was talking I was looking up the word "franchisor" in my dictionary. I had never written an operations manual before, but that was beside the point.

The man said he had to deliver an operations manual to each of his franchisees, and while he knew what the manual should cover, he didn't know how to write it. He said he could share the information with me in a matter of a day or two, and then he hoped that I would write it.

"Why do you have to deliver this manual to your franchisees?" I asked, stumbling over the word *franchisees* because it was almost foreign to me. I didn't know any franchisees. I had never discussed franchising with anyone before.

"The manual tells the franchisees what to do. It's sort of like a textbook. It provides guidance to the franchisees. If they follow the manual, they'll know what they have to do to build a successful business," he explained.

I was intrigued by the notion that anyone could build a successful business by following a textbook. "But how do you get the information that goes into the manual?" I asked.

"It's in my head," he said.

When I didn't respond he figured out that I was confused.

"The manual will describe my business," he continued. "Many people would like to do what I'm doing; they'd like to replicate my business. I need the manual to tell them what to do step by step. If they follow my directions, they can build a successful business, too."

"*Really?*" I said. I was as much amazed that this concept existed as I was that anyone could build a business by following a manual.

I was not a member of the Business School, but of the School of Communications. I didn't come from a business family, and even though I was surely interested in earning more than the $1,000 a month the university paid me, I would never have considered buying a franchise. But only because I didn't know such a thing existed.

I knew that McDonald's, Burger King, and other fast-food restaurants were franchises, but I never thought about how they worked. I didn't know there were opportunities to become franchisees. Or if I knew it, I dismissed it because surely you'd need $1 million dollars to become a franchisee.

"What's it cost to become one of your franchisees?" I asked. I knew he was about to ask me how much I'd charge to write the manual, so I needed to know what a manual was worth.

"Just $8,000," he said. "But as soon as I have the manual, I'm going to increase the fee to $12,000."

"How certain are you," I continued, "that this manual will do what you think it will do?" I just wanted to be sure that I understood the process, especially now that I knew a manual was worth $4,000.

"Are you saying that people will build a successful business by following the manual?"

"I'm guessing you don't know about franchising," he said.

"I don't," I admitted.

"If you'll come and spend a day or two with me, I'll teach you about franchising," he promised. "Maybe I'll turn you into a franchisee."

"I don't know about that," I said. "I'm not a business guy, I'm a writer."

"Yeah, but that's the beauty of franchising," he said, as he swung into his sales mode. "It doesn't matter what you are or what you do. It's all about what you want to do."

"But if I got into a business," I said, "I don't think I'd want to be in the food business."

He laughed. "You think franchising is just about McDonald's?"

"Well, it's about food," I said.

"Will you come and see me this Saturday morning?" he asked.

"I will," I said. "But before we hang up, what kind of business are you in?"

"Co-operative direct mail advertising," he stated, as though it was the only business to consider. "I'll explain it to you when I see you."

The simplicity of franchising

And that's how I met the late John Kinch, who franchised TriMark, one of the earliest business-to-business franchises. Today, you know the concept as Valpak or Money Mailer. Every month or so, they mail an envelope full of coupons to households across the U.S. and other countries.

When I met Kinch, and he told me how franchising worked, I was still amazed, but not as much now by the concept of franchising, but by the simplicity of the idea.

"You're telling me," I said, as we sat in his conference room at TriMark headquarters, "that if I pay you $8,000, you will tell me everything I need to know to build a business like your business?" He had already told me how much he earned from his business, and it was four times my university salary.

"You'll tell me where I should open the business. You'll tell me how to get clients. You'll show me, step by step, what I need to do to mail coupons to households in my business territory . . ."

"All that and much more," he assured me.

He promised to introduce me to several existing franchisees, and as he did, I interviewed them to gather more information for the operations manual that I agreed to write. Interestingly, none of the franchisees had ever previously worked in direct mail advertising. They all came from different professions, including teaching.

Suddenly, I was absorbed by franchising, and even though I wasn't prepared at the time to become a franchisee – I didn't have $8,000, and I still had several years left to complete my doctorate – I started telling people about my discovery and encouraging them to become franchisees.

Here's how franchising works

"It's a simple concept," I said over and over. And by this time I had discovered there were other non-food franchises in printing, sign making, auto repair, tax preparation, and cleaning, to name just several industries.

"You pay a fee – that may be the biggest challenge – and the franchise company trains you. They show you what to do. If you follow the operations manual, and listen to the franchisor, you'll succeed," I continued.

"Instead of you figuring out how to build a business from ground zero, someone shows you how they did it. You don't have to worry about developing brochures and advertising – they've done that for you. They tell you how to set up your office.

"They tell you how to get clients. They tell you how much to charge for your services. It's all done for you. They call it 'following their success system.'"

And, of course, in the case of TriMark, I documented that success system by writing the company's operations manual, the first of many that I would create during the next several decades.

Eventually, Kinch and I co-authored *Franchising: The Inside Story*, the first book written about how to buy a franchise. For that book, I interviewed approximately 100 people including franchisors, franchisees, franchise attorneys, and members of the International Franchise Association in Washington, D.C.

The process of writing that book gave me a deeper appreciation for franchising, and especially for its simplicity.

A concept for almost everyone

To this day, I tell people that franchising is a simple concept that almost anyone can use to develop a successful business and to create financial independence. Thousands of people do so every year, not only in the U.S., but in communities worldwide. There are now at least 3,000 different franchise opportunities in North America alone, meaning that just about every type of business has been franchised.

"Wait a minute," people will say to me. "If it's so simple, and if it's so fabulous, why have so many people failed? Why have so many people lost fortunes trying to succeed as franchisees?"

Many of these people will go on to tell me about their neighbor, or their relative, or someone they used to work with who bought a franchise and lost it all.

"But that doesn't mean it isn't a simple concept," I counter. "If it works the way I explained it to you, and I know from personal experience that it does, it's a simple concept that has led countless people from average lives to luxurious lives. You can't deny that."

Yet, some have lost fortunes

And I don't deny that people have lost fortunes – some may even have lost their lives – trying to build a successful franchise despite doing what a franchisor told them to do. I have written about those people in blogs, magazine articles, and books. I have met them at seminars, webinars, and during my coaching calls.

I know better than to say franchising is for everyone. But I maintain that franchising is a simple concept that builds wealth for people who understand why it works and how it works, and – most importantly of all – who acknowledge several fundamental tenets that define franchising in a near-perfect world.

Unfortunately, some people, some of the time, try to turn franchising into something it was never intended to be, and that's when franchising is likely to become a disaster. That's when the guy down the street buys a franchise and ends up in bankruptcy. Or the couple across town complain on a website, or in their local newspaper, about their franchisor, who is suing them.

In these cases, however, we rarely get the real stories. The guy who filed bankruptcy never mentioned that he refused to follow the franchisor's success system. He didn't confess to insisting on doing things his way, which turned out to be the wrong way. And the couple across town omitted the fact that they were selling unauthorized goods from their franchise outlet, which resulted in the franchisor's lawsuit.

Negative publicity creates fear of franchising

Every year in America, the most advanced franchise economy in the world, there may be hundreds of negative headlines and woeful stories in all forms of media about franchising, and if nothing else they create confusion about this simple concept that so many people have used to create fortunes.

Franchise critics, often themselves failed franchisees, look for the negative publicity and add their own two cents, as if dumping on franchising makes them more important. Among the misleading and erroneous points they want you to believe are these:

"Franchisors are out to get you."

"The franchise agreement is stacked against you."

"You're just buying a job when you become a franchisee."

"You can't make your own decisions when you're a franchisee."

"As soon as you start making money, the franchisor will find a way to slap you down."

"You don't own anything when you're a franchisee. You're just a pawn of the franchisor."

"You'll never be able to sell your franchise."

The criticisms are often nothing more than unsubstantiated nonsense, but they serve a purpose.

They create fear!

An acronym for False Evidence Appearing Real, FEAR stops people from buying franchises, or it at least slows down the process.

For more than 25 years, I've taught *The A to Zs of Buying a Franchise* at the International Franchise Expo in the U.S., and at other expos across America and abroad. At the start of every class, with 100 to 300 prospective franchisees in attendance, I always ask the same question:

"Why haven't you already purchased a franchise?"

The answers vary from not knowing how, or not knowing enough, or not knowing which one to buy, to not knowing how much a franchise will cost, or what a franchisor will require, or how much profit one franchise will generate.

But the common denominator among all of these answers is *fear.*

People should be afraid of franchising

If people are totally honest they'll say, "I'm afraid. I'm afraid I won't have enough money . . . I'm afraid I'll choose the wrong one . . . I'm afraid the franchisor will cheat me . . . I'm afraid I won't follow the franchisor's success system . . . I'm afraid I'll lose everything I invest and more. I'm afraid people will laugh at me for even thinking that I could build a profitable business."

And they should be afraid!

As I wrote in *7 Dirty Little Secrets of Franchising*, there are secrets that franchisors don't want you to know; secrets that they are not legally required to share with you.

Some franchisors, depending on the circumstances, will intentionally withhold information from prospective franchisees, just as some franchise salespeople will withhold information because they need to sell franchises. Salespeople, after all, usually get paid only when they sell a franchise.

Even some law-abiding franchisors may unintentionally withhold information that could make a difference in a franchisee's business performance.

Franchise agreements are very specific and long-term. Once you sign a franchise agreement, you become liable for what may be many years of financial penalties if your business fails. In fact, even if you keep your business open, but it under-performs, you may never generate enough income to feel rewarded for your investment and efforts.

Without knowledge and respect for the fundamental tenets of franchising, you should be fearful of franchising because it can take you down and under. Of course, without knowing and respecting the fundamental tenets of franchising, you are *not* qualified to buy a franchise, but it's unlikely that all franchisors will tell you that, especially if you want to buy a franchise.

If you've got the money and the desire, you can easily find someone to sell you a franchise regardless of your qualifications.

There's no Plan B in franchising

But before you make a decision to buy a franchise, you should know that while it's a simple concept, it's not a hobby. Franchisees don't have a Plan B. It's not like multi-level marketing where you can spend a little money, play around with it for a while, and then forget about it if the business doesn't catch hold. As one seasoned CEO of a major fast-food franchisor said, "Being a franchisee isn't a job you can quit —it's your life."

And it can be a great life! In a scenario where you do your part to succeed as a franchisee, you can use franchising to build independent wealth that buys you a lifestyle that you'd never achieve as someone's employee.

If you succeed, you can own one or multiple franchises, even multiple concepts of franchises, and you can accomplish the most fabulous goals imaginable.

When all the stars line up in the franchise universe, franchising erupts economically. It creates not only wealth, but a depth of personal gratification that rewards both franchisors and franchisees and the people associated with them.

With nearly 40 years invested in franchising – as an advisor to franchisees and franchisors, as a franchisee on multiple occasions, and as a franchisor of a major American brand – I've witnessed the eruption more than just a few times since that day when I spoke to John Kinch by telephone. When it works, and there's no good reason why it ever should not work, franchising is the envy of the business world.

And still, it's so simple!

It's a concept that works for many people, but it will not work for all.

The question now:

Will it work for you?

In the pages that follow, I'll tell you about the fundamental tenets of franchising. More than anything else I can think of, following these tenets is the best way to take away the fear of franchising.

You can then decide for yourself if franchising will work for you.

PART II
Know Thyself Because the Franchisor Might Not

Franchise Tenet #1:
Every franchise requires specific skills and values from franchisees.

Unless you understand the first franchise tenet, and how it applies to you and the franchise you intend to buy, you won't succeed as a franchisee. You may not fail, but any success you achieve will be the result of constant struggle, frustration, and ongoing aggravation between you and your franchisor.

In my opinion, offered as both a former franchisor and franchisee, there's nothing more important than this first tenet. If you miss this, you should be fearful of franchising because it's likely to destroy your life.

You may love a particular franchise opportunity or brand. It may be the "hot" franchise concept of the decade. Everyone says not to miss it! You may even feel passion for owning and operating the business and selling the product or service.

But if you buy the franchise without possessing the specific skills and values shared by the top franchisees in that brand's network, you're walking yourself into a nightmare that won't end for years!

Based on countless interviews with disgruntled franchisees, I feel relatively certain that a majority of franchise failures could be avoided if people accepted just this first franchise tenet. It's *that* important!

But many people miss it altogether. Prospective franchisees, as well as many franchisors, do not know that it's important.

Making matters worse: When you buy a franchise, it's *your* responsibility to be certain that you can provide the specific skills and values required by the franchise, even if the franchisor doesn't explain those skills and values to you.

Shouldn't the franchisor tell me that?

"Wait a minute," I hear you interrupting. "Doesn't the franchisor have some responsibility? Shouldn't the franchisor tell me if I've got what it takes to succeed as a franchisee?"

Yes, but . . .

First, don't assume that all franchisors are aware that skills and values matter, or even that these franchise tenets exist. The Franchise Disclosure Document does not require a franchisor to tell you what skills and values you'll need to succeed as a franchisee.

Franchisors are not required to pass any exams. They don't have to take a test in Franchising 101, for example, so they can't be held accountable for what's not expected of them. Franchisors are not licensed. No one checks up on what they know about how and why their franchisees succeed. Or fail.

In the United States of America, a franchisor becomes a franchisor upon producing a Franchise Disclosure Document and a franchise agreement, the two documents required by federal law. In some countries, franchisors become franchisors when they decide to sell franchises!

Until a franchisor gains experience – which almost always will occur after at least a few franchisees have failed – there's little opportunity for the franchisor to study franchising as a profession. And even then, many of the 3,000 to 4,000 franchisors that exist in North America don't know that they should!

Franchisors don't have to tell all

Second, don't assume the franchisor wants you to know *everything* before you agree to become a franchisee. I'm not at all suggesting that franchisors want you to fail. I've worked with hundreds of franchisors internationally, and I've never known one to sell a franchise with the expectation that the franchisee would fail.

However, franchisors are in the business of selling franchises. *Don't miss that point.* If franchisors don't continue to sell franchises, many of them could not pay their corporate bills, including rent and salaries. As part of your due diligence before you buy a franchise, you'll want to find out how much of the franchisor's revenue is generated by franchisee royalties as compared to initial franchise fees. Franchisors that operate from royalty flow are generally financially more secure than franchisors that must sell franchises just to pay overhead. But put that assignment aside for now.

The majority of franchise companies in North America include fewer than 100 franchises! Many franchisors live off the initial franchise fees they collect. Consequently, they cannot stop selling franchises. So even if they know the specific skills and values required of franchisees, they may not want to tell you. And just so they can sleep at night, they may not even want to know if you possess those skills and values!

Franchisors tell themselves that they'll teach their franchisees what they need to know during their basic training course. But some skills can't easily be taught, and many skills revolve around natural talent, and no franchisor teaches talent. You've either got it or you don't.

In addition, by the time you're old enough to buy a franchise, your values already exist. You formed those values over many years of life. Even if a franchisor teaches values – most do not – if your values don't mesh with the values required by the franchise, you're in the wrong business!

Franchisors don't always know their franchisees

Third, don't assume the franchisor has identified the specific skills and values required of franchisees. Sadly, franchisors don't know their franchisees.

I often ask franchisors to tell me about the skills and values of the franchisees who produce the most revenue for them. In other words, the franchisees who pay the highest annual royalties.

Most can't do it!

What do the top-producing 10 to 25 franchisees have in common?

What are their personalities?

What do they do better than the lower-performing franchisees?

Most franchisors have to think about those questions before they can answer, and even then some are just guessing. It's shameful, because they're taking your money with at least an implied promise that they know that you can succeed as a franchisee.

What's more shameful: There are numerous programs that franchisors can easily and inexpensively utilize to determine, up front, the skills and values of their top-producing franchisees, but most don't use them!

Ask for the documentation

I recommend that you buy a franchise only from a franchisor who has documented the skills and values possessed by top-producing franchisees. You should expect the franchisor to share this information with you and to show you the documentation, perhaps during a Discovery Day.

Before you buy a franchise you need to know the skills and values shared by the top-producing franchisees.

What are their capabilities?

How do your capabilities compare?

Here's what's going to happen. Shortly after you begin operating your franchise, you're going to wonder how your business compares to the other franchisees in the network.

Are you performing at the top of the network?

The bottom?

Or are you stuck in the middle?

After six months to a year of operating a franchise, if you're anywhere but the top, or at least steadily climbing into the top ranks, you're already in trouble.

And sadly, neither you nor your franchisor may know that you're in trouble!

If you're not at the top, you can feel it. For one thing, you're frustrated because the business isn't producing the money you had anticipated or the level of satisfaction. Besides that, the business is no longer as much fun as it was when you started.

But neither you nor your franchisor knows what to do to make your life better.

When you express your frustration or dissatisfaction to the franchisor, you may be told that your business needs additional time, or, you need to do a better job of following the system. Both answers could be true.

Or both answers could be stall tactics because the franchisor doesn't know what else to say.

If it's true that your business needs more time, or that you need to follow the system more closely, you can make some adjustments and you should see your business improve.

But it's possible – and very likely – that you're not where you expected to be as a franchisee because you *don't* possess the specific skills and values of the top-producing franchisees.

Save yourself!

And if that's the case, you've only got a couple of choices to preserve your sanity, and your money.

(1) Find out what's missing and hire! Maybe your franchise needs a sales person and you're not that person. Many people who buy franchises don't want to be salespeople. Or maybe you're not doing the best job of hiring and managing staff. It's important to realize that you can hire people to do the work that you don't want to do or can't do. And the sooner you hire, the better. Some franchisors are good at identifying early trouble spots and they can help their franchisees take corrective steps to turn a business around. Yes, of course, hiring staff will cost money that your franchise currently can't justify financially, but you've only got one other choice.

(2) Sell the business! In many situations, selling the

business and taking a loss is your best choice. If you don't have the skills and values that the franchise requires, and you can't hire staff because you don't have the money or you don't want to hire staff, then your best choice is to sell the business. No franchisee at this early stage of business ever wants to hear that advice, but it's better to cut the losses now and avoid digging a deeper hole. Countless failed franchisees — now bitter, former franchisees — wish they had taken this option. By the way, many mismatched franchisees, as well as franchisees who realize they can't turn their business around, helped create a business for FranchiseResales.com. It's a good place to find existing franchises for sale.

Selling your business for a loss is the hard way to discover that you lacked the skills and values needed to succeed as a franchisee in a particular franchise. You should never be put in that situation. Make it a point *not* to end up in that situation.

Passion is overrated

Don't let anyone tell you that skills and values are not important so long as you are *passionate* about franchising or about the brand. Franchise sales people often say they look for *passion* when they sell franchises. They say that passionate franchisees will overcome all obstacles and succeed.

To that I'd say: *Prove it!*

I don't think I've ever coached a franchisee prospect who wasn't passionate. As a former franchisor, I can't remember ever meeting a prospective franchisee who wasn't passionate. When people are in the process of buying a franchise with hopes of changing their lives for the better, they're naturally *passionate*.

But passion is no guarantee for success, and I don't know of any studies that prove that passion is even an indicator of success. If it were, there would be far fewer failed franchisees.

Skills and values also do not guarantee success, but a franchisee who brings the right skills and values to a franchise opportunity is at least positioned for success.

The HomeVestors story

Want proof? Let me tell you about my experiences at HomeVestors of America, Inc.

The late Ken D'Angelo founded HomeVestors – the "We Buy Ugly Houses" company – in Dallas, Texas in the late 1980s. Like most franchisors, he started franchising with a hope and a prayer, and not much money. He often talked about HomeVestors' first training class. While the training director led the franchisees through Lesson 1, he was in his office writing Lesson 2!

When I met Ken he had fewer than 50 franchisees. He asked me to help him strengthen his training program and to develop better support systems for franchisees. Of course, he didn't have any money to pay me!

So we worked out a plan whereby I was awarded a HomeVestors franchise in partial payment for the work I was about to do. At the time, I had no idea that Ken and I would bond like brothers, and that eventually I would succeed him as president and CEO.

Since I had no intention of operating my HomeVestors franchise, I recruited a partner who handled the day-to-day operations, which essentially included looking at "ugly" houses, buying as many of them at a deep a discount as possible, repairing them, and then putting them on the market for sale.

While I never worked in the business, I spent a lot of time talking to my partner to gain an appreciation for a franchisee's trials and tribulations. That information helped me as I completed various tasks for the company.

I also learned directly from Ken. We spent countless days and nights together during which time he talked about his passion: buying ugly houses, making them pretty again, and selling them for a profit.

Prior to franchising HomeVestors, Ken was one of America's top real estate investors, but he focused on Dallas, his home market. Ken had the heart of a teacher, which is perfect for a franchisor. Even if you had decided not to buy a HomeVestors franchise, but you wanted to buy and sell investment properties, Ken would still go out of his way to help you.

The ugly billboard story

Of course, Ken had the "secret sauce" that no competitor ever managed to copy, and without it no other company could do much harm to HomeVestors, which explains why HomeVestors was the only real estate investment franchise opportunity in the U.S.

Even though every media expert told Ken that a billboard was the worst possible means of advertising to buy houses, Ken paid a company to put up a colorful billboard that read: We Buy Houses 1-800-44-BUYER.

And just as Ken had predicted, the phones rang nonstop! However, too many of the callers wanted to sell their house for full price, and Ken was only interested in investment properties that he could buy at discounted prices.

So his next marketing decision convinced everyone, including family members, that he had lost his mind. He changed his colorful billboard to read: We Buy Ugly Houses 1-800-44-BUYER.

Everyone said the word "ugly" was insulting and therefore no one would call. Who would admit they owned an ugly house?

But once again, Ken proved everyone wrong. The phones continued to ring!

Within a matter of a few years, and with franchisees and billboards across several dozen states, HomeVestors generated 250,000 phone calls annually from people who wanted to sell "ugly" houses. Those leads were worth millions to real estate investors, but Ken shared the leads only with his franchisees!

Unfortunately, Ken was diagnosed with a deadly cancer and died in 2005 in his late 50s. "Don't worry about me, John," he told me just days before his death but while still managing to sit behind his desk. "I'm getting out of here, and I'm sticking you with the job that killed me!" He kept his sense of humor until his very last breath.

Who's making money?

At the time of Ken's death there were some 200-plus HomeVestors franchisees, and while Ken knew every one of them, I didn't. So one of my first requests of the HomeVestors' accounting department was to prepare a list of franchisees rank ordered by the number of houses they had purchased in the previous 24 months. They also were rank ordered by the amount of money they had paid HomeVestors in the previous 24 months.

In particular, I wanted to know the names of the top-producing franchisees, but I also wanted to know where every franchisee ranked in our network.

Fortunately, Ken had insisted that every franchisee complete a personality profile, the results of which helped Ken and his support team manage the franchisees when they ran into problems. The profile depicted a franchisee's personality traits (their values, and to some extent their skills) by colors:

"Red" signified a dominant, impatient, results-oriented, risk-taking personality. These were salespeople!

"Yellow" signified the life of the party! The "yellows" were informal, friendly, approachable and eternally optimistic. These were "people people." Everyone loved yellows!

"Blue" signified a creative, deep-thinking personality that often appeared to be aloof but was actually a stickler for details. These were big-picture problem solvers!

"Green" signified an informal, emotional personality that liked standards and systems but worked at a little slower pace than the other colors. These were detail-oriented problem solvers!

Whose got what it takes?

Which of those colors do you think depicted the right skills and values for success as a HomeVestors franchisee?

It will help you to know that a successful HomeVestors franchisee had to be able to tackle numerous tasks quickly, and sometimes simultaneously. But nothing happened in a HomeVestors business until someone bought a house, so that was mission #1.

However, it took courage not only to buy a house at a discounted price but to buy it from a widow who had raised a family in the house for 62 years and couldn't afford to live there anymore. Even if a fair price was embarrassingly low, a franchisee had to be willing to make the offer and stand by it. Padding the offer to make the seller feel better might result in the franchisee ultimately losing money! This was not a business for the faint of heart.

And when the seller said yes, the franchisee had to be prepared to move quickly to get the house under contract and to know what to do with the house. Franchisees had several choices:

(1) **"Flip" the house to another investor.** That was usually easy money! A franchisee could quickly grab $5,000 to $25,000 flipping a house. However, in order to flip a house, a franchisee had to know which investors were interested in that neighborhood or that type of property. Then they could assign the sales contract to the investor and collect a finder's fee.

(2) **Repair the house and keep it as a rental property.** Not every franchisee wanted a rental portfolio because rentals came with their own set of problems, which could be costly. But some franchisees bought a franchise with the sole purpose of building a rental business.

(3) **Repair the house and sell it to a new homebuyer for full market value.** That was potentially the big money maker! But it took time, and it was costly. Whereas a franchisee could put money in his pocket practically overnight by "flipping" a house, repairing the house and putting it on the market delayed the payday. And if the house didn't sell, the franchisee got stuck holding it along with an expensive mortgage.

From the moment the phone rang — giving the franchisee an opportunity to buy a house — delaying decisions was not in the franchisee's best interests. HomeVestors franchisees were well trained, and they had a terrific support network at the corporate office, but ultimately it was their business, and it prospered or failed depending on their skills and values.

While no one decision was likely to make or break the business, the culmination of decisions over a prolonged period separated the top franchisees from the lower-rung franchisees, as well as those stuck in the middle.

Managing personality profiles

When it came to buying a house, we favored the "red" personalities. They were bold, courageous, and quick to act. They showed no fear when they needed to buy a house at an embarrassingly low price. They were also good at selling houses at a premium!

But when it came to repairing and selling a house, we favored the "blue" personalities. They were methodical and systematic. They worked at a slower pace than the "reds," but they were good at getting repairs completed while also cutting costs.

For financing a house and for managing relationships with lenders, as well as contractors, we favored the "green" personalities because they were informal and sociable. They focused on building relationships.

As charming as they could be, the "yellow" personalities worried us the most. They could befriend other franchisees, as well as contractors, but the "yellows" often got carried away with their own importance, or they created expectations that neither they nor the franchisor could fulfill.

We knew the specific skills and values required of successful franchisees. For the most part, our franchise sales team, which included a former and an existing franchisee, had done an excellent job recruiting franchisees with the appropriate skills and values.

However, the rank-ordered lists showed me that we had some problems.

The top-producing franchisees were all "red" personalities. Not a surprise. Some of them were buying more than 100 houses annually!

But the franchisees at the bottom of the list, and in the middle of the network, were every color except red!

The franchisees at the bottom of the list weren't buying houses, and most of them were complaining. Some of them hadn't bought a house for months, which meant they weren't making any money for HomeVestors, or for themselves, and that was the basis for many of their complaints.

All of the franchisees received the same training. New franchisees were assigned seasoned coaches from our corporate office. We offered regional and annual meetings, so we had a strong support system. Our marketing – especially because of the billboards – produced off-the-charts results.

A franchisee might complain that he wasn't getting good leads, or his territory was "different," but that merely meant he wasn't a "red" personality. "Red" franchisees took their leads and ran, and they came back with results. If there were houses in their market, there were buying and selling opportunities.

Other colors simply didn't know how to treat their leads, and by the time they figured out what to do with them, their competition had already bought the house!

This sounds like we should have sold our franchises only to "red" personalities, but that wasn't the answer. Few personalities are exclusively one color, and as much as we depended on the "reds" to get things done in our franchise network, the "reds" could be a management nightmare. They were often socially bankrupt. They didn't care who liked them, and they weren't interested in making friends. They cared only about results. If they spent a dollar on marketing, they expected a $100 return! If they didn't get it, it was the franchisor's fault.

And besides, even though nothing happened until someone bought a house, much of a franchisee's work had to be done *after* buying a house. "Reds" were not good about cultivating relationships with other investors. They didn't want to spend their evenings at investor meetings and socials. If they were leaving their house, it was to buy another house!

"Reds" were also not the personalities to put in front of bankers and other lenders because they lacked discipline, and they said whatever came to mind. Similarly, homebuyers who wanted to take their time walking through a house, or imagining what they might do with a house if they bought it, also frustrated "reds." Contractors were not fond of "reds," especially if they were "red," so the ideal HomeVestors' franchisee wasn't "red."

The ideal HomeVestors franchisee was predominantly "red" plus one or two other colors, preferably "green" and/or "blue." But those folks were difficult to find. Besides, all colors were attracted to HomeVestors, and by the time I had become president and CEO we had an abundance of franchisees who lacked "red" in their personalities. And they were in trouble.

The good news was: We knew it!

And we were able to do something about it providing the franchisees cooperated with us. Many were, so when we told them they needed to hire a "red" personality to boost their buys, or they needed to attend a buyer's boot camp to improve their skills, they listened. In other cases, franchisees weren't capable of learning the skills of a buyer, and they couldn't afford to hire a buyer, so I offered our sales team to help them sell their franchises. Some did, but others ignored the advice.

Ultimately, you may recall that the real estate bubble burst by 2008, and real estate investment suddenly lost its appeal. That same year, we sold HomeVestors, and I left the company in early 2009. To this day, I'm still in contact with many current and former HomeVestors franchisees, including my franchise partner. It's no surprise that those who survived the Great Recession were mostly "red" personalities with touches of "green" and "blue."

Thanks to the late Ken D'Angelo, I learned the importance of matching skills and values to a franchise opportunity. I regret to say that many franchisors have yet to learn this lesson. If you choose to invest in a franchise opportunity where the franchisor doesn't recognize that skills and values make a difference, you're not just taking a huge, unnecessary risk, but you have every reason to fear for your future in that franchise.

How to protect yourself!

At every step of the buying process, I recommend that you protect yourself and don't expect anyone else to look out for your best interests. Just as franchisors can use tools to identify the skills and values of their franchisees, you can use the same tools to identify your skills and values. While you're exploring franchise opportunities, explore your personal talents by submitting to a personality assessment.

One of the most convenient assessments, and the one that I've used in my seminars and coaching programs for more than 25 years, is called DISC. You can complete this assessment in about 15 minutes online. When you access DISC via this link: surveymonkey.com/r/howtobuyafranchise, it's free. Better yet, once you complete the assessment I'll send you a personalized summary of your results, and that, too, is free.

Armed with this information, you'll also get a good idea of the types of franchise opportunities that make sense for you to buy. Later in this book, when I discuss the due diligence that you need to complete before buying a franchise, I'll remind you to ask franchisors and franchisees to help you compare the results of your personality profile with the requirements of the franchise opportunities of interest to you.

Hopefully, before you buy a franchise, your franchisor of choice will show you documented proof that your skills and values meet the skills and values required by the franchise. Without proof of this franchise tenet, you need to know that you're taking a bigger risk than any franchisor should expect.

One thing's for certain when you buy a franchise: If you want to protect yourself, you must know yourself. You can't depend on franchisors, franchise brokers, or franchise sales people to know you before buying a franchise.

Make sure you're clear about your skills and values, and then challenge the franchisor to prove to you that your skills and values are compatible with the franchise opportunity.

A franchisor who truly wants to sell a franchise, and who wants *you* as a franchisee, will accept your challenge. And you'll have one less reason to fear franchising.

Franchise tenet #1 is the most critical test you'll face before buying a franchise. As you continue reading, you'll find additional tenets in Part III, and once you understand them, and commit to them, your fear of franchising may disappear altogether!

PART III

Commit to These Franchise Tenets, If You Can

While the first franchise tenet is indeed the most critical, this chapter includes four additional franchise tenets to help you clearly understand what it means to buy and own a franchise. If you understand these tenets, and you're willing to accept and commit to them, only then should you buy a franchise.

And you can do so almost without fear of franchising.

Surprise, it's called business!

I say "almost" because in any business there's always something to worry about. Let's be realistic. In business there are always surprises!

You open your franchise on Monday and on Wednesday the city announces that traffic that would normally pass in front of your business will be rerouted for road repairs. And the repairs will take at least 90 days!

Or you think your franchise is doing well financially, only to discover that an employee cooked your books!

Or just as you were beginning to attract customers, a franchise competitor opens across the street and promotes lower prices!

If those routine issues are going to give you headaches, or deter you from opening a business, you may not need to read about the tenets of franchising because those issues are not franchise related. They're business related, and every business, franchised or not, faces them.

If you can't handle the surprises, don't open a business, franchised or not.

What is a franchise?

So what makes a franchise different from other kinds of businesses?

For many people, the first thought that comes to mind: McDonald's. The most famous franchise of all.

But McDonald's is a brand. It's a brand that achieved fame primarily because it's a franchise.

So again: What is a franchise?

- *A franchise is a license.*
- *It's also a methodology.*
- *And finally, and most importantly, it's a system.*

Franchise Tenet #2:
A franchise is a license.

Seems strange to think of it this way, but a franchise is represented, at least legally, by a piece of paper.

Brand owners – franchisors – choose to franchise by *licensing* to others – franchisees – to operate a specific business, in a specific location, in a specific way, for a specific period of time.

All of those *specifics* are vitally important. Don't miss any!

As a franchisee, you are awarded a license to operate a

brand, such as McDonald's, ServiceMaster, KFC, Mr. Rooter, or Signarama, etc. The license is called a franchise agreement, and it's signed by both the franchisor and the franchisee. The agreement establishes the terms of the franchise operation. We'll come back to that later.

While a franchise is a license, the act of franchising means something else.

Franchise Tenet #3:
Franchising is a methodology.

Franchising is a means by which a brand expands its locations, or builds more units, for the purpose of gaining wider distribution of its goods and services.

McDonald's uses the franchise methodology to build new locations and to sell (distribute) millions of hamburgers every day, along with French fries, milkshakes, and other products.

Signarama uses the franchise methodology to place its brand in communities across America where people who need to buy signage and related products can easily access the brand.

Other business methodologies

Franchising is one of several different methodologies.

In the U.S., your local Starbucks is not a franchise even though it looks and acts like one. Starbucks Corp., and not independent operators, owns those locations. Same for major department stores like Macy's and big-box stores like Target, Wal-Mart, and so on. These brands are corporate owned, and that's a different methodology.

Amway is a famous brand, but it uses yet another methodology – multi-level marketing – to expand and distribute products and services. Hundreds of other brands use multi-level marketing, or network marketing, as well.

In North America, some 3,000 to 4,000 brands, or companies, have been identified as franchises. They chose franchising as their distribution methodology.

So keep in mind that when you become a franchisee, even though you might identify with the brand, your ultimate responsibility is the distribution of products and services. Pretty simple, isn't it?

And the more you distribute, the more money you and the franchisor are likely to earn!

Franchise Tenet #4:
Every franchise is a system.

Distribution doesn't come naturally in franchising. It's a well-thought-out process that the franchisor is responsible for developing.

And as a result, *every franchise is a system.*

Correction: Every good or great franchise is a system.

In fact, the reason businesses fail is for lack of a system or a series of systems. It's the same reason most franchisees fail.

Knowing what to do when you're in business is a huge advantage. Would it surprise you to know that most people who start a business independently don't know what to do?

People will tell you that when you start a business the most important thing you need is money. I used to tell people that, too, because I foolishly believed what I read and heard. It was only when I experienced the real world that I changed my mind.

You can have more money than you need to start your

business, but if you don't know what to do, when to do it, and how to do it your business will eventually fail. Or at least it will under-perform.

An operating system, or a series of systems, is like business insurance! And that's really what you want to acquire when you buy a franchise.

Savvy franchisors spend countless hours and money to document their systems, which may include an operations system, an advertising system, a customer-service system, a profit system, etc.

When you buy a franchise, the franchisor loans you (it's never yours to own) that series of systems and provides you with training and support relative to each system.

The systems should provide real answers, (i.e. tested answers), to all of your questions about operating your business, including:

- Where, specifically, to locate your business, keeping in mind that the location must be perfect for attracting customers but also not so expensive that it eats your profits.

- How to buy the best equipment and supplies for your franchise, and utilizing the franchisor's quantity discount.

- Where to buy signage, and where to place signage in your business.

- How to hire, train, motivate and fire employees – without getting sued.

- How, when and where to advertise and promote your franchise, utilizing materials (i.e. radio and television commercials, print ads, social media promotions, etc.) provided to you by your franchisor. Unless you know how to create an ad, or launch an online promotion, it's never a good use of your time trying to do so because you're going to waste money!

- What to say to a prospective customer to turn that person into a paying customer who returns to your business week after week. Few businesses knew how to upsell – *Would you like fries with your burger?* – until McDonald's taught us how.

- Understanding your profit and loss statement. If your business generates money every month, why aren't you able to take more of it home? Look specifically at your percentage of sales spent on rent, employees, cost of goods, cost of customer acquisition, etc. If those percentages are out of whack, you're losing money!

In the process of buying a franchise, the franchisor says to the franchisee: "Here's my system. For a fee, I'll let you use it to build a satisfying and profitable business. However, you must use it *my* way, and you must agree to never change it without my knowledge. Fail to comply, and I'll take back my system and keep any money you paid to me."

That's the deal.

Don't like it? Save yourself the agony. You don't have to fear franchising to say no to it. But you do have to respect it.

It's the franchisor's license and the franchisor's systems, and only the franchisor has the right to award franchise licenses.

Yes, the franchisor is in control.

Franchise Tenet #5:
The franchisor is always in control.

This is a challenging tenet for many prospective franchisees because they want to be in control.

I hear you saying, "Look, I've been in a career for 12 years working for someone who told me what to do when I knew how to do it better. There's no way I'm going to buy a business and not be in control."

Fair enough.

Do yourself a favor: Don't buy a franchise.

If you do, you're going to be miserable. That's because, in most situations where control is the issue, the franchisor trumps the franchisee.

If you ignore this tenet and you buy a franchise expecting that somehow someway you'll gain control, you should be very fearful. Not to be fearful in that case is very stupid, and I won't apologize for being so blunt.

Go back to the second tenet. *A franchise is a license.* Re-read the paragraph that says a franchisor licenses a franchisee to operate a *specific business, in a specific location, in a specific way, for a specific period of time.*

How to operate the business specifically is clearly detailed in the franchise agreement. You as a franchisee are required to sign that agreement and thereby commit yourself to the deal terms.

The agreement doesn't specifically say you are giving up control, but it spells out all the situations in which you don't have control.

For example:

- You can't open the business wherever you want and operate it whenever you want. You think you're closing on Christmas? Or never working on weekends? Think again.

- You can't sell anything that's not pre-approved by the franchisor. You may discover a new product that you could take to market before any competitor, but you can't legally sell it unless your franchisor approves.

- The way you represent the franchise brand, including how you and your employees dress and what you say to customers, is pre-scripted and not up to you.

- How and where you advertise isn't up to you, either. Neither is the amount of money you can spend on advertising.

And so it goes.

If you fail to comply with these controls, you have already agreed, by signing the franchise agreement, that the franchisor has the right to penalize you, including taking back the license without refunding any money to you.

Why would anyone buy a franchise?

Wow!

You must be thinking: *Knowing all that, why would anyone buy a franchise and give away all that control?*

Allow me to share one good example that explains why people should be willing to give away control when they launch a business. I'm sure there are countless stories just like this one, but this one I know personally.

Years ago in my home state of Ohio, my cousin, Mary Jo, and her husband, Tony, decided to open a pizza shop. They were young, energetic, and entrepreneurial, and they had a small sum of money to invest in a business. Tony was already part owner of a successful business with his brothers, but he and Mary Jo wanted something to build for themselves.

Selling the Best Pizza Ever!

For years people had been telling them that they made the

best pizza ever, and no wonder because they both grew up in the kitchens of Italian mothers. "You should get into business and sell these pizzas. It's the best pizza ever!" friends told them over and over.

So when it came time to start something of their own, my cousins decided to get into the pizza business. They had plenty of money to buy any one of the famous pizza franchises, but they knew that if they joined a franchise they'd be forced to use the brand's pizza recipe and not be able to use their own recipe, which produced "the best pizza ever."

And since the purpose of getting into business was to sell "the best pizza ever" – or so it was for them – they didn't consider buying a franchise.

As they went to work on their own, they found a shop, they sourced the equipment, they bought a sign, they acquired supplies and materials, and they began making pizzas.

And for a while, they were busy because all of their friends came for pizza, and friends told friends about Mary Jo and Tony's new pizza shop with "the best pizza ever!"

But then, as always occurs with a new business, the flow of customers slowed down, and my cousins were faced with some decisions. They didn't deliver pizza, and their shop didn't include many tables, so they relied mostly on customers calling to order a pizza and then coming to pick it up. By this time, however, all the pizza franchises delivered pizza, and customers preferred home delivery, if only for the convenience.

"We can't afford to deliver pizzas," Tony explained to me one day. "The insurance alone is sky high. Plus, figuring out the delivery routes is complex." So they decided not to introduce delivery. If customers wanted "the best pizza ever" they'd have to come and get it.

That was Strike One.

A good pizza franchisor would never have allowed them to get into the pizza business without delivery.

While my cousins had a large circle of friends, and their friends influenced their friends, a business won't survive on friends alone.

"We hadn't done any advertising when we opened the place," said Tony, "but now we knew we needed to get the word out."

He looked at a variety of options – the Internet and social media had not yet been introduced – and for whatever reason, he decided newspaper advertising was the way to go. But it was expensive!

And it was ineffective for selling pizzas.

That was Strike Two.

A good pizza franchisor would never have encouraged Tony to advertise his store in a newspaper. Pizza franchisors know that newspaper advertising – even years ago when newspapers were more popular – isn't effective for selling pizzas.

Logically, in a town with only one newspaper, but a newspaper that was popular and widely read, what better vehicle was there than the daily newspaper for promoting "the best pizza ever?"

Sometimes, as franchisors will tell you, logic makes no sense in business. In fact, look at any of the successful pizza franchises – and there are many, with new brands introduced almost every year – and you won't find even one that uses newspaper advertising as its primary means of marketing and promotion.

Instead, the folks who cracked the secrets to selling pizza

figured out that pizza customers don't stray far from home, especially if they've got to drive to the pizza shop to eat or take away the pizza.

Chances are pretty good that most of a pizza shop's sales comes from within a 2- to 5-mile radius, depending on the density of population. The radius will be larger, but not much larger, for a shop that delivers pizza.

Do people who read newspapers buy pizzas? Certainly.

But is newspaper advertising the most cost-effective means for a pizza shop to attract customers? Certainly not.

What works?

Door hangers!

Instead of paying huge sums of money for newspaper ads, Tony and Mary Jo should have printed thousands of flyers and arranged for a company, or a team of part-timers, to deliver to every house within three miles of their shop a flyer with a coupon. That's what a pizza franchisor would have advised at the time.

"Tonight, try the best pizza ever!" Location and phone number included on the flyer along with a map. Total cost would have been far less than newspaper advertising, and the sales impact would have been immediate.

If Tony could have told the newspaper to insert his advertisement only in newspapers that were delivered to the houses within a 3- or 4-mile radius of his shop, the advertising might have paid off.

But that's not what the newspaper offered.

Tony's ad for "the best pizza ever" would be seen by people who lived just down the street from the pizza shop, but also by people – in fact, the majority of people – who lived 20, 30 even 60 minutes across town.

And they weren't going to fight traffic for a pizza. Not when there were a dozen pizza shops between them and Tony's location, and not when they could get a pizza delivered to their home in 30 minutes or less!

But it wouldn't be "the best pizza ever."

And there was Strike Three.

A good pizza franchisor would never have encouraged Tony and Mary Jo to produce "the best pizza ever" because it wasn't necessary. The pizza franchisor, with dozens of successful franchisees, had already proven that a better recipe doesn't make a difference.

Long, long ago, Americans made it clear that they do not require or demand the "best pizza." It's not that they don't want it or crave it, but they're not willing to pay for the "best pizza," or be inconvenienced to get it. The same goes for hamburgers, cookies, frozen yogurt, ice cream, pancakes, and other food products.

"The best pizza ever" wasn't only inconvenient for most people to buy, it also cost a little more than other more-famous pizzas because of the ingredients.

The higher cost might also have been due, at least a little bit, to ignorance.

"How many slices of pepperoni can you put on a large pizza and still sell it for a profit?"

Hmmm. No one had thought about that. Well, the top pizza franchisors have.

And Mary Jo and Tony, solo operators, had to pay premium prices for all of their ingredients and materials because they were buying for just one shop.

Meanwhile, their competitors, franchisees of famous

and not-so-famous brands, paid considerably less when they purchased flour, cheese, and pepperoni, because they took advantage of their brand's economy of scale. Suppliers are willing to lower their unit prices to provide products for a 500-chain brand or a 1,000-chain brand, but no supplier gives a discount to solo operators.

Another business failure

It took some time for Strike Three to deliver its fatal blow, but not before Mary Jo and Tony had depleted their savings. In spite of "the best pizza ever" – and it truly was – their business was a failure.

What's even sadder is that the failure could have been predicted and prevented.

They could have bought a pizza franchise, and if they had, their children might be selling pizzas yet today.

No, they wouldn't be selling "the best pizza ever," but then that begs the question: Is the purpose of a business to sell the best of something? Or is it to accomplish something else?

For example: The purpose of a business is to satisfy, if not exceed, customer expectations so that the business thrives financially.

If you can accomplish financial success *and* sell the best of something then you've struck a goldmine. But in societies where people are comfortable saying, "It's good enough," or "It's convenient," business often isn't about selling the best of something.

If people won't pay for "the best pizza ever," or won't even consider buying it because it's inconvenient, why would you start a business around that recipe?

A good pizza franchisor knows better.

Successful pizza franchisors – and the same is true of all successful franchisors regardless of the industry – don't get hung up on selling a product because of its personal history or even because people say it's "the best ever."

Even the best of friends, offering the most objective of opinions, don't necessarily understand the dynamics of starting, building and maintaining a successful business. They may know good pizza when they taste it, but they don't necessarily know business.

Franchisors learn via trial and error

But successful franchisors do. Some of them have had to learn the hard way themselves. Some of them have invested millions of dollars to test ideas, to develop business systems only to fail, and then revamp the systems and start over again, and again.

Successful franchisors rarely begin a business knowing how to market, advertise and promote their products, but through trial and error – and buckets of money – they figure it out.

They discover how to find customers, how to treat customers, and they become proficient at serving customers, knowing their limits, knowing what they will buy, and understanding their behaviors. They know, better than most operators, why customers buy what they buy!

And then the best franchisors document everything. That's how they create systems, and training and support programs. Through their experiences they know what's required to replicate their business. If they're really good – and many are not – they also know the type of person who will succeed as a franchisee.

And that's why people buy franchises.

They're paying for systems, training and support, but they're also buying knowledge and experience. And controls.

I can only wish that Mary Jo and Tony had ignored their friends. If selling pizza was really what they wanted to do – and clearly it was not – then I wish they had bought a franchise, controls and all. It not only would have saved their investment and saved their business, it might also have saved their marriage, and her life.

Before it was all over, Mary Jo and Tony's fairytale romance ended bitterly. No one could even fathom how two people, so in love and seemingly so right for each other, were suddenly at each other's throats, but a failed business will do that to the best of couples.

And then, worst of all, closing out the nightmare, Mary Jo was diagnosed with breast cancer and didn't survive after several years of agony.

I have no proof that a franchise would have made the difference, or kept them together and kept her alive, but it doesn't take a scientist to know that the boiler cooker they were in, the loss of funds, the embarrassment of business failure, and the stress of it all took its toll.

As it turns out, when it came to franchising, they had nothing to fear so long as they understood the tenets of franchising, so long as they vetted franchisors to find a good fit, and so long as they were willing to accept a franchisor's seemingly onerous controls.

Control versus freedom

So it comes down to this. Control versus freedom. Do it the franchisor's way, even if the end result isn't the "best" of something, or do it your way.

But know this: If you do it your way, you're probably going to fail.

Meanwhile, you now understand five critical franchise tenets that explain why franchising is successful. A franchisor grants a license to a franchisee to operate a business, that is, to distribute products and/or services, and provides the training and support so the franchisee learns how to successfully implement the franchisor's systems and ultimately build a profitable and satisfying business. All the while, the franchisor remains in control.

If you can accept these tenets, you have fewer reasons to fear franchising. But there's still the matter of accepting the risk of starting a business, and that's the subject of the next chapter.

PART IV
Can You Accept the Risk of Starting a Business?

I thought of titling this book: *Take the Fear Out of Business* because when you buy a franchise, you buy a business, and if you're fearful of franchising, you've got to be fearful of business.

Take the Fear Out of Business would surely appeal to a wider audience and sell more books, but then I would likely miss the majority of my primary audience, people like you, who want to buy a franchise.

Besides, when it comes to the fear of business, a book that you absolutely must read is Michael E. Gerber's *The E Myth: Why Most Businesses Don't Work and What to Do About It.* For years I have only half jokingly said that the U.S. government should require prospective business owners to read Gerber's book before granting them a business license. Franchisors are well advised to make the book required reading and include it in their franchisees' training curriculum.

Gerber didn't write the book to address the fear of business but rather to explain how a business should be organized for success. Essentially, a business should be organized like a franchise, whether or not it's going to be franchised, and to organize it any other way would merely hasten the demise of the business and generate a financial loss for the owner. Of course, most people do not heed Gerber's advice and consequently the chances of starting a business and succeeding in America are grim. For that matter, they are grim everywhere in the world.

Look at these business stats

You have good reasons to be fearful of starting a business, but they are not the same reasons that make you fearful of franchising. In recent years, business failure rates have gone from bad to worse, according to the U.S Bureau of Labor Statistics.

U.S. businesses founded in 2006 had a 49.3 percent chance of survival, *down* from 55.3 percent in 2003. The 10-year survival rate for businesses founded in 1998 was only 37 percent. We don't know how many franchised businesses were included in the data used by the U.S. Bureau of Labor Statistics.

According to the U.S. Small Business Administration's (SBA) Office of Advocacy, about half of all new businesses survive five years or more in America, and about one-third survive 10 years or more. It would be interesting to know if franchised businesses fared better or worse than non-franchised businesses, but the SBA does not differentiate that data. However, you'll soon discover that that differentiation doesn't matter all that much anyway!

Gallup explains business risks

In 2015, an article by Gallup's chairman and CEO, Jim Clifton, pointed out that starting a business in America is more perilous than ever. Relying on data provided by the U.S. Census Bureau, Clifton explained:

"Business startups outpaced business failures by about 100,000 per year until 2008. But in the past six years, that number suddenly reversed, and the net number of U.S. startups versus closures is minus 70,000."

And if that's not bad enough . . .

"For the first time in 35 years," Clifton wrote, "American business deaths now outnumber business births."

With those statistics, could anyone draw down their life savings to start a business, franchised or not, without at least a little bit of fear?

Is it any wonder that many people who dream about starting a business can't because they're confused, dazed, and/ or immobilized?

No specific info about franchises

Interestingly, while the U.S. government doesn't break out data that's specific to franchising, the government treats franchises as businesses, albeit small businesses, and expects franchisors and franchisees to comply with a myriad of business laws. Collectively, franchising is "big business," though its numbers pale in comparison to non-franchised businesses, or what Gallup refers to as "America, Inc."

There are some 6 million businesses in the United States but only some 800,000 business-format franchise units (not including gasoline stations, auto dealerships and bottling companies). Throngs of lobbyists at all levels of government protect America, Inc., while franchising mostly depends on one association, the International Franchise Association (IFA), and individual franchisors and franchisees, to do its lobbying.

IFA mobilizes groups of franchisors and franchisees for local and federal grassroots lobbying, but lacking the gobs of money that millions of big businesses pay out for protection, franchise lobbying is high-spirited but not always effective.

9 million franchise jobs!

Nonetheless, no one should overlook that franchising provides nearly 9 million jobs and creates jobs at a faster pace than the overall economy!

Franchising is a force that Congress and the government cannot ignore. The loss of franchising would deliver a devastating blow to the American economy, not to mention destroy the dreams of successful franchisees and their franchisors.

Traditionally, the U.S. government has mostly ignored franchising. But in 1979, the U.S. Federal Trade Commission (FTC) promulgated what is now the most onerous Franchise Rule worldwide, which dramatically changed franchising in America for the better.

Franchise "bandits" on the loose

Franchising gained popularity in the 1950s with a burgeoning post-World War II economy, but charlatans disguised as franchisors appeared everywhere and took advantage of unsuspecting consumers who thought they might build their own financial empires, or at least build thriving small businesses, by owning a franchise.

The criminal elements appeared at business opportunity expos where they were permitted to sell their so-called "franchises" from the expo floor. Sales presentations were loaded with fabricated stories that promised wealth to the next person who paid a small deposit of just a few thousand dollars. The deposit reserved a space for the payee in the franchisor's next training program, which never occurred. The bandits escaped with the money in the still of the night, leaving behind fake business cards. There was nothing anyone could do about the losses except complain to anyone who would listen.

Interestingly, real franchisors, honest franchisors, listened! They, too, exhibited at business opportunity expos, and they watched the criminals at work. Before it got worse, they intended to do something to stop the bad guys from destroying a business concept that, properly implemented, really could help people build their own wealth while creating jobs and businesses.

Creation of International Franchise Association

A group of legitimate franchisors, fed up with the charlatans, rallied around William Rosenberg, founder of Dunkin' Donuts, and formed the International Franchise Association (IFA) in 1960. Their first priority was to get the attention of state and federal legislators to enlist government assistance to clean up franchising. Even at that it would take nearly 20 years before the federal law was issued.

Due to these efforts, franchising has become a legitimate business choice with built-in mechanisms to protect consumers. Ironically, consumers are not required to avail themselves of the government's protections, and they frequently do not for any number of baffling reasons, such as, "I didn't have time to do the due diligence because I needed a job" or "I had no idea the franchisor's disclosure document was intended for me to read; I gave it to my attorney" or "My brother-in-law said it was a good deal and I believed him," etc.

Nowadays, thanks to the IFA, it's unlikely that anyone who serves in the U.S. Congress, and even in the state legislatures, doesn't at least know about franchising as a legitimate business choice. Every year in Washington, D.C., the IFA organizes franchisors and franchisees in small groups that descend upon Capitol Hill for the purpose of meeting with legislators and their staff members to educate them about franchising. They also make them better aware of the trials and tribulations of franchisors and franchisees in the hopes that they will keep their plight in mind when they amend regulations or introduce new laws.

None of this activity, however, has moved the federal government to treat franchising in a formal way. In addition to the FTC, the SBA treats franchising as a legitimate business choice, and provides many resources for both franchisors and franchisees, but there's no office anywhere in the government – it would make sense within the SBA – that tracks franchise developments.

The Kostecka Report

But that was not always the case. Many years ago, a civil servant who worked for the U.S. Department of Commerce surveyed franchisors and then compiled his findings in a report titled *Franchising in the Economy*. The booklet appeared annually through most of the 1980s.

To my knowledge, no one ever knew how Andrew Kostecka, assigned to the Bureau of Industrial Economics, conducted his research, or how he extrapolated the results that he reported in *Franchising in the Economy*, but the report was widely distributed among franchisors and the media, and the results often quoted.

On one occasion in 1989, while Mr. Kostecka was in the midst of collecting data from franchisors, I visited him at his Washington, D.C. office and he showed me numerous surveys that had been recently completed by franchisors and returned to him via mail or the office fax machine.

I was fascinated to review the handful of surveys, but I was in no position at the time to evaluate the data or the collection process, or ask questions about how he formulated his final report. I hadn't expected to discuss his research when I visited him because he had invited me to lunch and he suggested that I stop by his office and then we'd walk together to a nearby restaurant.

Several months earlier, Andy and I had become friends when we traveled together to Japan with a group of franchisors organized by the IFA. For years, Andy had facilitated trade missions that included as many as a dozen franchisors who, in return for a fee paid to the government, traveled together to visit foreign markets in hopes of selling their franchise rights to a local investor who would then expand the American brand locally.

When President Ronald Reagan downsized government services in the 1980s, Andy was forced to give up the trade missions and also cease publishing *Franchising in the Economy*.

Rather than lose valuable opportunities for franchisors to expand internationally, the IFA picked up the trade mission business, and to my great benefit appointed me to promote the trade missions at home and abroad. Shortly thereafter, I found myself in the company of Andy Kostecka, man of the world, and a small group of franchisors that regularly traveled with the trade missions.

In no time I noticed that when Andy spoke, people listened! For one thing, he towered over most people. He had played basketball for Georgetown and was selected in the 1948 draft by the Indianapolis Jets, but retired after one season. He joined the U.S. Army, worked for the Central Intelligence Agency and ultimately the Department of Commerce. The combination of Andy's winning personality and his vast experiences made him the Big Man on Campus no matter where he went.

When Andy spoke to government officials and reporters in London or Tokyo or Frankfurt about the emergence of American franchising and the benefits his touring group of franchisors could bring to their city and nation, everyone listened. For a dozen or more years, Andy Kostecka was U.S. franchising's greatest spokesman. In fact, no one in the world at the time influenced more people about the benefits of franchising.

Survival rate of franchises

Part of Andy's research for *Franchising in the Economy* focused on the "survival rate" of franchises, and that information was widely circulated, discussed and quoted. It's fair to say that of all the data Kostecka reported, the "survival rate" won the attention of franchisors because it helped them sell franchises. And remember: The franchisors provided the data!

According to Kostecka's research, "97 percent of franchises survived!" When he reported that statistic, which he did with the unstated endorsement of the U.S. Department of Commerce, no one seemed surprised. In fact, everyone seemed to accept that statistic as a fact and no one questioned it.

If someone asked Kostecka what he meant by "survived" – a reasonable question – he explained that he asked franchisors to report the number of franchise agreements that were in effect last year, and the number of those same agreements still in effect a year later.

On a number of occasions I heard him tell a reporter, a franchisor, or a group of his colleagues in another country, that he was looking for the "discontinuance rate" of franchises.

If a franchisee had signed a franchise agreement in June

1985, and the franchisor reported that that agreement was still in effect in June 1986, then the franchise had "survived."

Kostecka was quick to add that he was not using survival as a measurement of success, but he didn't think it was far-fetched to assume that if a franchise agreement survived, and especially if it survived for multiple years, that the franchisee was likely enjoying some degree of success.

Of course, the franchisee was never consulted, and the data collection relied solely on the franchisor and the franchisor's integrity. Surely some, and maybe most, franchisees represented in the study enjoyed success, whatever that meant.

One franchisee earning $35,000 a year may have considered his enterprise a success while another franchisee would be disappointed not making 10 times that number. Of course, while some franchisees were successful, at least some were barely making ends meet, or they were borrowing money just to keep their business afloat. Meanwhile, their franchise agreement remained in tact year after year!

All that data didn't mean much

The point is, except for the franchisees and possibly the franchisors, no one really knew what all this meant. No doubt there were franchise companies that had never experienced a failure. As unlikely as it seems, it still happens today. A franchisor may go for many years without a franchisee failing, and when the failure occurs it may or may not be the fault of the franchisor. Again, no one really knows, except the franchisee and the franchisor, and usually they won't say.

For Kostecka's part, he was merely doing what he thought a good civil servant ought to do: return value to the taxpayers. He witnessed franchisors developing business concepts and brands that average people could acquire for modest amounts of money and then replicate with some training and support provided over time by the franchisor.

Kostecka always admired tenacity and hard work – hallmarks of successful athletes as well as franchisors – and many of the franchisors became his personal friends. Occasionally he may have been too trusting and too friendly; he may have overstepped some boundaries now and again, but no one who knew Andy Kostecka doubted his intentions. He was a winner who wanted to help other people win, too.

Good intentions, however, couldn't erase the flaws in Kostecka's data or his conclusions, and even though the government stopped publishing his reports more than a quarter of a century ago, his infamous "survival" statistic continues to pop up on franchise websites even today.

Kostecka didn't study franchise success

Except now, the word "survival" frequently has been replaced with the word "success." It's as though the bandits are back again! Or they never went away. These are the guys who will tell you that the U.S. government "proved" that 97 percent of franchises succeed!

Of course, the government said no such thing.

Ever.

Which begs the question: *Is it safer to buy a franchise?*

About.com apparently thinks so. That website reported: "Some studies show that franchises have a success rate of approximately 90 percent as compared to only about 15 percent for businesses that are started from the ground up. The increased probability of success usually far outweighs any initial franchise fee and nominal royalties that are paid monthly."

The rumble you hear is my old friend Andy Kostecka rolling in his grave at Arlington National Cemetery!

Franchising derailed

While during the 1980s *Franchising in the Economy* was widely reported as a triumph for franchising, and especially for franchisors, other books and studies surfaced in the 1990s and said it was all bunk!

If people got the notion that they could trust franchising in the 1980s, they got a more forceful message that they should fear franchising in the 1990s.

Robert Purvin's 1994 book, *The Franchise Fraud: How to Protect Yourself Before and After You Invest,* caught the franchise community unaware. Purvin's message essentially said that instead of a success story, franchising in America was a nightmare.

As an attorney specializing in franchise law and chairman of the American Association of Franchisees and Dealers (AAFD), which often positioned itself at odds with IFA, Purvin disputed the claims that franchising represented a safe and secure path to business ownership. He wrote his book to help consumers avoid becoming victims of what he called the Franchise Fraud.

Purvin's book was a wakeup call at a time when franchising was booming. Suddenly, despite the FTC's Franchise Rule, and despite the (fictitious) 97 percent "survival rate," the spotlight was cast on people who bought a franchise and got stung!

Like Kostecka, Purvin had the best of intentions, but unlike Kostecka, a champion of franchising, Purvin appeared to be a franchise doomsayer who was out to build his own legal practice and bolster the pesky AAFD, which at least appeared to pit franchisees against franchisors. It was an unfortunate scenario, especially because the good guys in franchising outnumbered the bad guys, but the latter group continued to make a mess of things.

The notorious Bates study

Purvin's book was followed by what may be the most notorious – and damaging – study of franchising. Dr. Timothy Bates, at the time an economics professor at Wayne State University, published a 1995 article in *Small Business Economics* that turned franchising on its head.

Titled *A Comparison of Franchise and Independent Small Business Survival Rates,* Bates' study examined – once again – survival patterns among franchise and non-franchise firms started between 1984 and 1987, and found that independent firms were more profitable and more likely to survive.

After four years, only 62 percent of the franchised businesses had survived, while 68 percent of independent small businesses were still operating. And the independent businesses proved to be more profitable. In fact, on average, profitability was negative for franchises represented in the study. Furthermore, the average capital investment of franchisees was $500,000 compared to $100,000 for independent entrepreneurs.

Ouch!

"Despite the hype that franchising is the safest way to go when starting a new business, the research just doesn't bear that out," said Bates.

Now the fear of franchising was real because an accomplished economics professor said so.

Through the 1990s and into the new millennium, various other surveys, studies, and books, as well as scathing media reports, have taken their shots at franchising, but franchising continued to not only stand its ground, but to expand.

Every negative report could be refuted by "experts," or at least explained by simply saying that the findings represented a mere snapshot of what was actually occurring in franchising at the time, or reflected economic factors (i.e. high interest rates, recessions, downturns) that occurred at the time.

Franchise buyers beware

For its part, the IFA firmly spread the message that franchising was no safe haven; if you planned to buy a franchise you better do your homework. The fear of franchising was real.

Even so, many people seemed oblivious to any message that even suggested a fear of franchising. They wanted to buy a franchise because they liked a certain brand. Or they wanted to buy a "hot" business. Or they needed a job, or a career. Or their neighbors or friends or in-laws were making big bucks with a franchise business and, bottom line, they wanted one, too!

However, there was something else going on that everyone missed, including franchisors and the media. Amidst the frenzy of who reported what about franchising, there was one fundamental explanation that would make all of this nonsense go away.

It didn't matter what Bates or Purvin or Kostecka said about franchising. It didn't even matter what the SBA, or any other government agency reported about the success or failure of franchisees.

If you understood just one principle, you could laugh at the survey results, the articles, the TV exposes, and the books that bashed franchising. While you cannot overlook the fact that starting a business is risky, you can minimize your risk if you follow just one principle. And in Part V of *Take the Fear Out of Franchising* I'll share that principle with you.

PART V
Pay Attention to the Only Data That Matters

As you prepare to buy a franchise, you are expected to do your homework, or what's formally called "due diligence." This is the process by which you "investigate" the franchise opportunity or opportunities that most interest you.

Unfortunately, many people fail Due Diligence 101. They either ignore it, they don't know how to collect the data, or they don't know how to analyze the data to arrive at reasonable conclusions.

Too many people go with their "gut feel" when buying a franchise: "I liked my salesman. I trusted him, and so I didn't feel the need to do any more investigating."

I've heard words similar to that statement countless times in the last 30-some years – always from disgruntled franchisees looking for a way out. They should have spent more time looking for the right way in.

If you take due diligence seriously, and I hope you do, this book provides guidelines to help you complete your homework or your own investigation of franchising and specific franchise opportunities.

You can do your own investigation, or you can hire

someone to help you, although I don't recommend the latter because ultimately the decision to "buy" or "not to buy" a franchise rests with you.

Do you really want to invest your life savings in a business that someone else told you to buy?

Or not to buy?

Every year, even though it's been more than half a century, I still hear people say they're kicking themselves for not buying a McDonald's franchise. "If only I hadn't listened to my neighbor."

No need to investigate franchising

Many experts, including consultants and advisors who you might engage, formally or informally, will tell you that step one of your due diligence must be an investigation of franchising as a concept, or as an industry, similar to the information that I provided in Part IV of this book.

But I am telling you that's a waste of your time.

In fact, you might be better off if you never knew about the studies and reports provided by Andrew Kostecka, Robert Purvin, Dr. Timothy Bates, and a host of others who have released positive and negative information about franchising during the past 30-some years. You certainly wouldn't be at any disadvantage.

For one thing, as soon as a report is issued, it's out of date. Its findings are based on data collected months if not years earlier, and most likely during different economic conditions. How relevant is it now?

Yes, of course, I believe we learn from history, and I believe that solid researchers can help us develop opinions and perspectives as well as identify trends. But telling us that most franchises succeed or fail is (almost) worthless information.

And here's why.

It's a squishy industry

No one knows for certain how many franchisor companies exist because franchisors are not required to register or to declare themselves as franchisors. Yes, every franchisor in the United States must file a disclosure document before selling a franchise, but no one's counting.

And you can be sure there are some businesses that sell franchises without filing a disclosure document, either on purpose or for lack of knowledge. These businesses may say they're selling "business opportunities," not franchises, but what they're actually doing is skirting onerous and costly franchise regulations, and most likely to the detriment of the people who buy from them.

But since no one keeps track of the number of franchisor companies, the best guestimates say there are some 3,000 to 4,000 franchisors in North America. The number expands annually. The International Franchise Association (IFA) says that new franchisor companies increase by about 10 percent every year. Of course, since no one officially tracks franchise companies, no one knows how many franchisor companies fail or close their doors each year.

Are you getting the idea that franchising is a squishy industry?

Some specific data about franchises overall does exist. For example, the IFA reports that nearly three-fourths (73 percent) of franchisors support fewer than 100 franchise outlets. Only 5 percent support 500 or more units, and 7 percent are still looking for their first franchisee.

Many people find those numbers surprising, if not shocking. Most franchise companies never grow larger than 100 units!

We also know that franchising as a methodology is used by businesses in 75 major industries, including quick-service restaurants (the largest sector), automotive repair, senior care, home services, construction, entertainment, financial services, etc. Some of the largest franchise companies are in the food and beverage industry, but some of the most successful franchise companies are in real estate, education, and business services, to name a few.

Get the relevant facts

Overall, franchising is best described as diverse. So how can anyone study the industry and report *relevant* data about success and failure to a prospective buyer? It's very difficult if not impossible to do. Even at their best, averages and national trends are interesting to read, but no one should use them to make a buying decision about a franchise.

If I told you that "most" franchises survive – a true statement – does that help you? There would still be "some" franchises that fail. You might think the odds are in your favor, and so while you're still a bit uncertain, you go ahead and invest your life savings in a franchise opportunity.

And two years later you're out of money and forced into bankruptcy. You can't understand it because, after all, "most" franchises survive.

Yes, they do, but you selected one that didn't. Assuming that you did everything right as a franchisee, it was just your "bad luck" that you selected the wrong franchise!

Or was it?

You can wrestle with the national data that the media report from time to time about franchising, or you can simply ignore it. Wise investors ignore it because it does not matter!

You must get this part right

But here's what you must not ignore: The success and/or failure history of the specific franchise brand you intend to buy!

That's a critical component of your due diligence. In fact, if you get this part right, you'll know whether or not you should buy a specific franchise brand, and you'll be confident about your decision.

Here's the good news: While it's unlikely that you can get specific data or scientific evidence, you can still determine the success or failure history of specific franchise opportunities. More than anything else you do, uncovering this information about specific franchise opportunities will take away your fear of franchising.

Once you get a franchisor's disclosure document, you can go to work to figure out the success versus failure history of that brand, and that's *relevant* data. It doesn't matter how *all* franchises perform across the board or within their industries. What matters is the performance of the *one* franchise opportunity that you hope to buy!

You may have to dig deep into a half dozen opportunities before you discover the right one to buy, based on the success-versus-failure history. But if you want to give yourself the best opportunity to succeed in franchising, there's no substitute for the work that needs to be done.

What franchise attorneys say

Hoping to find a shortcut to this critical information – success versus failure – and to uncover a scientific methodology for capturing the data, I interviewed two seasoned franchise attorneys who frequently help clients perform due diligence on franchise opportunities.

Warren Lee Lewis is chair of the Franchise & Licensing Practice at Akerman LLP in Washington, D.C. He is also a member of the North American Securities Administrators Association (NASAA) Franchise Project Group's Industry Advisory Committee. NASAA is responsible for facilitating compliance with franchise disclosure requirements under state franchise investment laws.

Cheryl L. Mullin spearheads Mullin Law, PC in Richardson, Texas, a Dallas suburb, and was recognized in Best Lawyers in America®, Franchise Law, 2007-2017, and named to Texas Super Lawyers®, Franchise and Distribution Law, 2011-2016.

I've known these attorneys for more than 30 years, and by all counts they are legal superstars in franchising. Interestingly, while I interviewed them separately on different days and without one knowing that I was interviewing the other, they both follow a very similar path in completing due diligence relative to franchise opportunities.

Both also agreed that while there's no scientific methodology for determining the success-versus-failure rate of a franchise company – at least not without the cooperation of the franchisor and its franchisees and an independent auditor to examine the data provided – prospective franchisees can still take several specific steps to get a handle on a franchise brand's success-versus-failure history.

Grab the disclosure document

The first step is to get a copy of the franchisor's current disclosure document, which includes 23 items of information to help you decide if this is the right franchise opportunity for you. While an attorney most likely prepared the disclosure document for the franchisor, don't worry. The document must be written in simple English. If you can read and understand this book, you can read and understand most of a disclosure document's content.

Federal law requires franchisors to provide an annually updated disclosure document to prospective franchisees prior to selling a franchise in the United States. Franchisors are not required to give a disclosure document to foreign investors, but many will do so simply because the disclosure document is the best way to explain a franchise opportunity.

A legitimate franchisor selling a franchise in the United States will not ask you to sign any binding documents or pay any money until you've had the disclosure document in your possession for a minimum of 14 days. You and your advisors, which may include an attorney, an accountant, and a franchise or business consultant, should use the contents of the disclosure document to help you form opinions and conclusions relative to the franchise opportunity.

Turn first to the financial statements

Lewis and Mullin both almost immediately turn to the franchisor's financial statements, Item 21, to get an advance idea of the franchisor's performance.

"I want to see whether revenues and profits are growing or declining," explains Mullin.

"I look at profit and loss," says Lewis, "to determine if

it's really a company. And if it is a company, and it's making money, what's it doing with the money? Are they taking every dollar out of the business, or are they using the money to reinvest in the franchise system?"

Both attorneys pointed out that they carefully read the notes that pertain to the financial statements. "Sometimes there is good information in the notes," says Mullin. "For example I just read a disclosure document where the franchisor said in Item 1 that it had no predecessors or affiliates in a similar business, but the notes to the financial statements talked about how the franchisor was a successor to some other company that was engaged in the same business."

For most of us, especially if we're not lawyers, it may seem tedious to read the notes at the end of a financial statement, but a good lawyer isn't going to gloss over any of the data in a disclosure document.

Charting a franchisor's performance

After examining Item 21, Item 20, Outlets and Franchisee Information, also provides early indicators of a franchisor's value, and both attorneys say it's important to pay attention to this section. The data in Item 20 is fodder for helping you determine the success-versus-failure rate of the franchise brand. However, studying the information will take time, especially if you're new to franchise due diligence, and you may want to engage one or more of your advisors to help you make sense of the information.

There are five charts in Item 20 and each (with one exception), covers a 3-year period:

(1) **System-Wide Outlet Summary** — shows the number of outlets owned by franchisees and by the company (many franchisors do not own any outlets);

(2) **Transfers of Outlets to New Owners** — shows the exchange of ownership that occurs when a franchisee sells to a new franchisee;

(3) **Status of Franchise Outlets** — shows the number of outlets opened, terminated, non-renewed, reacquired by the franchisor, and ceased operations;

(4) **Status of Company Owned Outlets (if any)**; and

(5) **Projected New Franchised Outlets** — shows the franchisor's growth projections by state.

Perhaps you quickly realized that Charts 2 and 3 are important indicators of a franchise brand's success-versus-failure rate. If the number of transfers is rapidly increasing, you'd want to know why. Is it because franchisees are failing? Not making enough money? Or are they unhappy with the franchisor?

If more franchise units are terminated than sold, or they're not renewed, or the franchisor is acquiring a large percentage of units every year, something's wrong with that franchise. These are all red flags that should prompt you to ask the franchisor for more information.

"You cannot use the data in these charts to get a percentage of success or failure," says Lewis, "but the charts reveal a snapshot of the franchise company. The data tells you if the system is growing or if there's been a lot of turnover of units, or if units are being terminated. In all cases, it's important to ask why. A lot of turnover may be occurring because the franchisees are not making money!"

Is there an earning's claim?

Item 19, Financial Performance Representations, is also an early indicator of success or failure, but only if the information is provided by the franchisor. This is the one optional item in the disclosure document. While franchisors are obligated to provide all other information required by the disclosure document, they do not have to file what's commonly called an "earning's claim." However, if they decide not to provide this information, they are prohibited from discussing earnings with a prospective franchisee.

Some franchisors, in fact, prefer not to discuss earnings, especially if they're unimpressive. So when you ask, "If I buy your franchise, how much money will I earn?" it's easier and safer for the franchisor to say, "I'm not permitted to disclose that information."

You might even hear a franchisor claim, "The law doesn't allow us to disclose earnings information," but that's not true. The law encourages franchisors to disclose earnings in Item 19 but does not force them to do so. Of course, critics of franchising think that's a bad idea, and franchisors should be forced to include financial performance representations, but at the moment, that's not the law.

"Most of the disclosure documents that I review disclose financial performance," explains Mullin. "Some are more detailed than others. Some disclose only gross sales numbers." And in that case, Lewis adds, where the franchisor doesn't include the franchisee's costs, you don't know if the franchisee earns a profit. While it's not unusual for new businesses to operate in the red for a period of time, if the business doesn't eventually break even and begin to operate in the black, it's most likely going to fail.

Other pertinent information

Disclosure Items 19 (if it's included), 20 and 21 are indicators of the franchise brand's success-versus-failure history, and the information in these items are all you need to take the next step as you complete your franchise brand due diligence.

However, lest you think the other items in the disclosure document are not important, I want to be sure to emphasize that all items in the disclosure document serve a valuable purpose. It's a mistake to think that you've completed your franchise brand due diligence without reviewing all of the items in the disclosure document. The document provides a comprehensive view of the franchise opportunity, and you can't claim to know what's expected of you without reading and understanding the document in its entirety.

For example, Lewis points out, "A lot of prospective franchisees don't understand that they will be paying fees for as long as they are franchisees." In fact, depending on the franchise agreement, a franchisee could be obligated to pay fees even after the franchise is closed and terminated!

Items 5 through 7 address the fees you'll pay, including the upfront franchise fee, the ongoing royalty, and, if required, the advertising fund fee. "I look at the initial investment and it's relationship to what the unit might earn," says Mullin. "Does the initial investment make sense in light of the anticipated return on investment and the market challenges?"

Item 8, Restrictions on Sources of Products and Services, tells you if you're free to buy from sources of your choice or if you must buy from sources owned by, or controlled by, the franchisor.

Item 16, Restrictions on What the Franchisee May Sell, tells you exactly that, while Item 12, Territory, addresses protected versus non-protected territories. Mullin says, "I look at territorial protections and restrictions. Can franchisees provide offsite services? Delivery and catering services? Sell on the Internet? The more freedom a franchise has to go out and develop a territory the more attractive" the franchise opportunity may be.

Both attorneys urge you to consider Item 3, Litigation, and Item 4, Bankruptcy, to determine the experience of the people who own the franchise company. "What kind of people are they?" asks Lewis.

Back to the nitty gritty: Success versus failure

While all of this is valuable advice that you should use as you complete your franchise brand due diligence, I recommend that you first focus on the success-versus-failure history of the franchise brand. Therefore, you should temporarily set aside all items in the disclosure document and focus on Items 19, 20 and 21.

I recommend that you prioritize your due diligence because until you know the success or failure history of a franchise brand, there's no sense worrying about the balance of the information in the disclosure document. You may decide not to pursue the opportunity based on your initial investigation.

Here's the goldmine

The information in Items 19, 20 and 21 will not in itself always provide conclusive evidence about the franchise brand's success-versus-failure history, but there's additional information in Item 20 that leads you to the next step of your investigation. In addition to the five charts, Item 20 includes contact information for current and former franchisees. *Voila!* This is your goldmine. You've still got to work the goldmine, but that's where you'll get the answers you desire and need.

The Franchise Rule requires franchisors to provide contact information for all current franchisees or for all franchisees in the state where they are offering to sell franchises, providing there are at least 100 franchises in that state. Since most franchisors never sell more than a total of 100 franchises, their disclosure documents reveal contact information for all of their franchisees.

Franchisors are also required to provide contact information for every franchisee whose outlet was terminated, canceled or not renewed, or the franchisee otherwise voluntarily or involuntarily ceased to do business under the franchise agreement during the most recently completed fiscal year.

These lists of current and former franchisees provide a neat database for you to continue exploring the success-versus-failure history of the franchise brand. All you've got to do is contact the franchisees and ask the appropriate questions!

In my best-selling book, *101 Questions to Ask Before You Invest in a Franchise*, I provide a comprehensive list of questions to ask franchisees, franchisors, franchise advisors and even vendors to franchise companies. Several of those questions pertain to the success-versus-failure history of the franchise company.

Don't forget to ask the franchisor

Even though we're now focused on interviewing franchisees, don't hesitate to tell the franchisor that you want to know about the company's track record. Before you begin interviewing franchisees, ask the franchisor: "What is the success rate of your franchisees?"

You may or may not get a useful answer. The response may depend on whom you ask within the franchise organization. You should expect a franchise salesperson and the company's corporate counsel to answer the question differently, and in either case the information may not be as helpful as you desired.

To be fair, it's not an easy question to answer, at least not without some explanation. The raw data, which you accumulated from the charts in Item 20, may be black and white (i.e., 100 franchisees opened businesses, and 20 of those franchisees closed businesses), and that may be all you want to know.

But a franchisor, regardless of the number of failures, high or low, will almost always want to provide some explanation, and it may be important for you to hear it. It's not unusual for franchisors to discover a weakness in their development or their training and support systems, and to their credit, they will make changes to prevent future disappointments, including failures.

"Ten of the 20 failed because they were under-capitalized and we didn't know it when we sold them a franchise," the franchisor might say, and honestly so. Since selling those franchises, the franchisor may have changed the financial qualifications for future franchisees or may have discovered a better way to verify a prospective franchisee's financial information.

"All but a few of them sold because they were ready to retire. The others sold because they wanted to buy other types of franchises," and that, too, may be an honest explanation.

But other explanations may not be as straightforward. "If they would have done what we told them to do none of them would have failed," the franchisor reports, and that, too, may be true, but not very helpful.

"They failed because they just weren't cut out for our kind of franchise," the franchisor may explain, harking back to franchise tenet #1: *Every franchise requires specific skills and values from franchisees.* Now's the time for you to ask the franchisor to explain those skills and values to you, to be sure you possess what's needed so that you can succeed in this business.

But what's the chance that if you interviewed the former franchisees they would tell you the franchisor didn't have clear-cut recommendations or any recommendations? Or that the franchisor never tested their skills or questioned their values? It's possible the franchisor had yet to develop a success system that worked.

And that's why you're asking these probing questions. You want to know if this is a legitimate franchisor with systems and solutions that will help you turn your investment into your personal fortune.

Vendors are another source of information

After the franchisor, the franchisees (current and past) are your best source for information about what's happening within a franchise network. Sometimes, however, vendors provide great insights, too, but they may not be as willing to disclose what they know for fear of losing an account.

Still, you can imagine what a vendor knows! A vendor knows a franchisee's sales volume based on what the franchisee buys from the vendor. A vendor that provides cheese to a sandwich shop or pancake mix to a restaurant or cones to an ice cream parlor knows the volume of products sold by the franchisee. Vendors also know how the volume fluctuates, perhaps by seasons. They also know which franchisees pay their bills on time, which may or may not be an indicator of success or failure.

If you can locate vendors – you can ask the franchisor and franchisees for their contact information – don't be afraid to interview them. As much as they want to protect their customers, they also want to protect innocent people from financial disasters. And they're not looking to take on new franchisee customers who aren't going to be able to pay their bills!

At a minimum, vendors can share with you pertinent information about territories, store locations, and other market factors that separate high-volume stores from low-volume stores.

Overall best source: franchisees

But ultimately, some of the most valuable information you can gather about the franchise opportunity, and in particular the success-versus-failure history, will come from franchisees, current and past. That's why savvy franchise prospects use the Item 20 database to complete their due diligence.

You can expect the Item 20 information about existing franchisees to be current, but information about past franchisees is most likely out of date. Franchisors are not required to keep track of past franchisees or to update their contact information. Phone calls and emails to previous franchisees will most likely not be answered. Oftentimes, these former franchisees do not want to be found or they do not want to discuss their past relationship with a franchisor. In some cases, especially if the two parties disagreed and arrived at a settlement, in or out of court, the former franchisee is legally prevented from discussing the relationship.

Finding former franchisees and engaging them in meaningful conversation is a challenge. My own efforts to find these individuals are rarely successful.

However, it's easy to contact existing franchisees and get them to agree to speak with you by phone, answer your questions via email, and/or welcome a visit from you to give you time to observe their business for a day. Once you demonstrate to a franchisee that you're a serious candidate – that is, you're reading or read the disclosure document, you qualify financially to buy the franchise, and you've attended the franchisor's Discovery Day, or you plan to – you'll find most franchisees to be helpful.

Franchisees reserve time for serious candidates

Franchisees are busy people and they don't want to spend time talking to "tire kickers" or people who are simply "dreaming" about buying a business but who have no idea of the expectations and requirements. They want to know that you've already done some homework. They're not obligated to talk to you, and they're not paid to talk to you (if they are, that information must be disclosed). Most franchisees are willing to give you their time and information because they share an *esprit de corps*. They want to be helpful. Besides, they may remember when they were in your shoes and they needed franchisees to help them.

Of course, franchisees also want to protect their brand. They want to be sure that you're not only qualified to buy a franchise, but that you're the type of person they would welcome into the franchise network.

You should expect that after talking to you or meeting you in person, the franchisees will report back to the franchisor to share their opinions, especially if they're unfavorable. Even if they're not asked for their opinions they'll report them because they care about the quality of the people who become franchisees.

In some cases, however, where franchisees believe that a new franchisee in their territory would only reduce their sales, it doesn't matter whether or not you're a good candidate. Those franchisees will campaign against you because they don't want additional competition. Ultimately, however, the franchisor is in control of deciding where and when to add franchise locations.

If you invest time getting to know franchisees, it's almost impossible not to find one or several who will take you into their confidence. They'll not only tell you the upside of buying and operating the franchise, but they'll tell you the downside, too.

Seasoned franchisees are most helpful

You might discover franchisees who are members of the brand's franchise advisory council. Ask the franchisor for the names of those franchisees or ask existing franchisees to point you to them. In their role as advisors to the franchisor and representatives of the franchisees, they're usually comfortable talking about the pros and cons of the business and about the performance of specific franchisees. They're not intimidated by the franchisor – as some new franchisees may be – and if they've been franchisees for many years, they know the company's success-versus-failure history.

If past franchisee failures were the fault of under-capitalized or rogue franchisees, advisory council members are likely to tell you so. If past franchisee failures were the fault of the franchisor – perhaps selling a bad territory or encroaching on a franchisee's territory or falling short in the areas of training and support – they'll tell you that, too.

Finding former franchisees

If it's important to you to speak to former franchisees, ask the existing franchisees for their contact information. Current and former franchisees often stay in touch – sometimes they're related! – so you can find former franchisees if you really want to. However, those franchisees may not be forthcoming with information, depending on how they ended their relationship with the franchisor.

Bottom line: Following the guidelines in this chapter, you can uncover the success-versus-failure history of any franchise opportunity. It's unlikely that you'll be able to calculate a percentage of success or failure, but you should *not* buy a franchise without at least knowing this information.

You can forget the national polls, surveys, articles and books that address the success and failure of franchises – they're meaningless – but if you carefully complete your franchise brand due diligence, you'll know what to do next. You'll either buy the franchise opportunity, or you will pass and look for another opportunity, making certain to complete your due diligence all over again.

And that's how you take the fear out of franchising!

AFTERWORD

Fear of franchising shouldn't be underrated. You've got every right to be fearful about investing your life savings in a franchise and committing yourself to a franchise network. For every success story in franchising, there also seems to be a horror story, and so you can't be too careful if you plan to become a franchisee.

But now, having read *Take the Fear Out of Franchising*, you know that it's possible to invest in a franchise and succeed. And now you're prepared to learn everything you need to know about franchising, and specific franchise opportunities, before making a decision about whether you should become a franchisee.

I hope you agree with me that it's a simple process. I hope you recognize the value of the five franchise tenets, and that, in particular, you pay close attention to your personal compatibility with franchising. Take advantage of my offer to complete a DISC profile and in return I'll send you information about your compatibility with franchising.

In the final analysis, franchising is a simple concept that works, and yet it's not for everyone. And it may not be for you.

If it is for you, then *Take the Fear Out of Franchising* is just a first step in your exploration. There's much work to be done. To help you, I've added several bonus chapters:

- *17 Steps to Successfully Buying a Franchise* leads you through the franchise acquisition process from beginning to end. You can think of this as a roadmap that guides your journey. I've also included questions you should ask along the way.

- *Funding Your Franchise Acquisition: Where Do You Get the Money?* This is an overview of the funding options that are available today. You may have all the money you need to acquire a franchise, or you may want to rely on banks, leasing companies, and even franchisors to assist you. Many people choose to convert their retirement funds into capital that they can invest in a franchise. It's controversial for some, but many have used it successfully.

- *Foreign Investors: Use Franchising to Get a U.S. Green Card* explains how some people are investing in franchises and franchise funds to create jobs in the U.S. The investor and his or her family are then entitled to live in the U.S.

- *Franchise Terms and Resources* provides information about franchise jargon and leads you to trusted sources of information and assistance.

Thousands of readers have also utilized my best-selling books: *101 Questions to Ask Before You Invest in a Franchise* and *Buy "Hot" Franchises Without Getting Burned* to complete their franchise due diligence. I'm sure you'll find these books useful, too.

Finally, my website, HowToBuyAFranchise.com provides hours of free information to help you investigate franchising and specific franchises. I've also produced many podcasts and videos that will educate you even further about franchising.

Everything you need to know about franchising, and about specific franchise brands, awaits you. Take your time, but set aside your fear for now because you know exactly what to do to find the perfect franchise opportunity – providing, that is, that franchising is right for you! I hope it is.

- Dr. John P. Hayes
HowToBuyAFranchise.com

17 STEPS TO SUCCESSFULLY BUYING A FRANCHISE

Everything is possible with a system!

Outstanding achievements are the results of someone following a system. With the right systems you can succeed at almost anything. What is it that you want? There's a system to help you get it.

You want to successfully buy a franchise? It won't surprise you, I don't think, to discover that there's a system for doing so. And here it is: *17 Steps to Successfully Buying a Franchise.* If you follow these guidelines, you're taking all the right steps to explore franchising, to consider the pros and cons of franchising, and, if franchising makes sense for you, to ultimately find a franchise opportunity worthy of your investment.

Even though I cannot guarantee your success as a franchisee – no one can because there are so many variables at play – if you complete these 17 steps you can eventually sign your name to a franchise agreement with the confidence that you've done everything possible to ensure your own success as a franchisee. Of course, you must follow the system and complete each step with integrity.

Based on that understanding, here are 17 steps to success-fully buying a franchise:

1. Educate Yourself

As you prepare to buy a franchise, spend time reading (or viewing informational videos) to make sure you understand what franchising is all about. You can also get good information at franchise conferences and through franchise advisors. One way or another, familiarize yourself with the fundamentals of franchising.

Questions you should ask:

- *Why is franchising so successful?*
- *What are the main reasons for franchise failure?*
- *How can I be sure that a franchisor is legitimate?*

2. Why Franchising Exists

Of all the points that you need to understand about franchising, the most important may be this: *Franchising is a system of distribution.* Franchising is a means for marketing and selling products and services. Don't get caught up in any of the hype about franchising. Yes, of course it's a way for you to own your own business, and it may be the safest way to do so, and it may be your ticket to financial independence, but do not overlook the fundamental purpose of franchising: *It's to sell stuff!*

Questions you should ask:

- *Am I excited about distributing the franchisor's products and services?*
- *Do I see myself operating this system for five, 10, or more years?*
- *How can I be sure that the franchisor's system will work in my territory?*

3. Does Franchising Make Sense for You?

Be absolutely sure that franchising makes sense for you. Franchisors are not interested in selling franchises to the wrong prospects or investors. You should be equally as protective of yourself. Ask the question: *Is franchising for me?* Keep in mind that it's not for everyone. If it's not for you, don't force it. Read Part II of *Take the Fear Out of Franchising.* Utilize the DISC personality profile – it's free!

Questions you should ask:

- *What qualifies me to be a franchisee?*
- *Why do I want to be a franchisee?*
- *What type of franchise will make the most sense for me?*

4. Know Your Role as a Franchisee

Understand that the franchisor creates the *system* and the franchisees follow the system. Good franchisors know what needs to be done day to day, month to month to succeed in the business. And that's what they'll expect you to do. Everything you're required to do is part of the system, so you must be willing to follow it, even if you don't always agree with it. Otherwise the franchisor can take away your franchise. The franchise agreement mandates that you follow the franchisor's system.

Questions you should ask:

- *How can I learn more about the franchisor's system?*
- *What aspects of the system may or may not be of interest to me?*
- *Do existing franchisees endorse the franchisor's system?*

5. You're Buying a License

By legal definition, a franchise is a license. A franchisor licenses a franchisee to operate a specific business in a specific manner at a specific location (or in a specific region) for a specific period of time. The license can be renewed and either party also can terminate it. Be sure you understand those details before you invest.

Furthermore, the franchisor retains ownership of (almost) everything! The franchisor's intellectual property, training materials, marketing methodologies, sales processes, possibly even phone numbers and clients, always remain the property of the franchisor and not the franchisee. These details will be explained in the Franchise Disclosure Document.

Questions you should ask:

- *What are the specific terms of the franchise agreement?*
- *Do I get a protected territory? (You may not want a protected territory and you do not necessarily need one, depending on the franchise.)*
- *What if I decide I want to sell the franchise; how do I do that?*

6. The Franchise Work Environment

Think about the franchise work environment. Most franchisors require franchisees to be owners/operators. In other words, you can't be an absentee owner. Some franchisors expect franchisees to work from home or a small office. Other franchisors require franchisees to work from a retail shop at a strip center or a mall. Other franchisors require franchisees to work from a van or another type of vehicle. In some cases franchisees work alone; in other cases franchisees manage employees. Once you know which work environment makes sense for you, pursue franchise opportunities that support your preferences.

Questions you should ask:

- *Do I want to manage people?*
- *Am I comfortable working alone, from my home or a small office?*
- *If I prefer one work environment but the franchise companies of my choice require a different work environment, can I adjust?*

7. Did You Know They Franchised THAT?

There are at least 75 primary industries that use franchising as their method of distribution. Once people explore franchises, they're surprised by the industries that have developed franchise opportunities. It's best to find the industry that makes sense for you. Keep in mind that from industry to industry, franchise investment costs vary.

Questions you should ask:

- *Which industries interest me the most?*
- *Which industries can I afford?*
- *Which industries provide me with the best opportunities?*

8. Look for the Right Opportunity

No one knows how many franchise opportunities exist, but estimates suggest there are 3,000 to 4,000 opportunities in North America alone. Many of these opportunities are local or regional, and some of the companies are sold out so they're not offering franchises except internationally. Some industries include a dozen or more franchise companies offering similar and competitive franchise opportunities, while other industries may only include a handful of franchisors. Of course, these numbers are of little consequence considering that you're looking for just one franchise – the one that's best for you. You will find these opportunities by reading books and articles, attending expos, and by being observant: What's being franchised today that interests you?

Questions you should ask:

- *How much money can I invest in a franchise? The answer may dictate the industries that you should explore.*
- *How do I want to spend the next five, 10, or more years of my life in business?*
- *When it comes to "selling stuff," what excites me?*

9. Information is Free; Ask for It!

When you find a company that interests you, ask for information. It's free, and it comes without any strings attached. Remember, a U.S.-based franchisor must provide U.S. citizens with a disclosure document at least two weeks before selling a franchise. The clock doesn't begin to tick until you acknowledge receiving the disclosure document. And franchisors will not send you that document until they've had an opportunity to speak with you and know that you are qualified to invest in their business. There's no reason not to ask for information, provided you're genuinely interested in the franchise. You can expect the company to ask you for your personal information before sharing information with you. Generally, a franchisor wants to get your email address, your phone number, the timeframe in which you plan to buy a franchise, and an understanding of how much money you intend to invest in a business. By the way, it's a mistake to provide misleading information – once you're found out, do you think the franchisor will trust you?

Questions you should ask:

- *Are you planning to open franchises in my territory of choice?*
- *How much is the investment in your franchise?*
- *What makes your franchise business unique and amazing?*

10. Read the Information Carefully

Invest time to carefully read the information provided by the franchisor. Make sure you not only can see yourself as a franchisee, but that you understand the business and the requirements of franchisees in your company of choice. The franchisor's preliminary information may not be specific, but the information in the franchisor's disclosure document must be specific. If you like what you're reading (perhaps even seeing, if the franchisor provides links to videos) plan to ask for the disclosure document.

Questions you should ask:

- *If I were to invest in this franchise, what else would I need to know?*
- *Is this a business that makes sense for my location, or territory?*
- *Where's this business headed in the next five to 10 years?*

11. Attend the Franchisor's Discovery Day

Visit the franchisor. Almost every franchisor sponsors a Discovery Day. This is your chance to visit the franchisor's headquarters, meet company representatives (possibly even franchisees), and learn more about the franchise opportunity by listening to a variety of presentations and asking questions. The franchisor may also include a tour to show you the training center, the marketing department, etc. Franchisors do not charge a fee for Discovery Days, but you most likely will be expected to provide your own transportation and lodging. However, don't be afraid to ask the franchisor to pay for your expenses, or to share your expenses. Depending on how eager the franchisor is to sell a franchise, you may get a free trip. But even if you have to shell out some money for this experience, it's worth it. If you're married, the franchisor may want your spouse to attend, too.

Questions you should ask:

- *How is this business unique and amazing?*
- *How does this business compare to similar franchises?*
- *What's the future for this industry, and this franchise in particular?*

12. Get Disclosed

Ask the franchisor for the Franchise Disclosure Document (FDD). Once the franchisor knows that you're a "serious" candidate to buy a franchise, by law the franchisor must "disclose" you before continuing to talk to you about the franchise opportunity. This is a very serious matter and franchisors are careful not to violate it.

When you ask for the disclosure document the franchisor will ask you for detailed information to qualify your candidacy. Be prepared to tell the franchisor about your net worth, your personal and professional background (including any criminal violations), and the timeframe in which you plan to buy a franchise. Expect the franchisor to investigate this information by running a credit history and a criminal background check. The franchisor may also require you to complete a franchise personality assessment.

Receiving a FDD does not obligate you to do anything! You must have this document for at least 14 days prior to buying the franchise. But you're not obligated until you sign the franchise agreement.

Questions you should ask:

- *How long has this franchise been in business; who owns it; how are the franchise company's executives qualified to be in their positions?*
- *How much training and support will I receive? Does it cost extra money?*
- *How often (if ever) have franchisees sued the franchisor, and why?*

13. Go to Work for a Franchisee

One of the most important steps you can take before buying a franchise is to talk to existing franchisees. Call them, visit them, and spend time with them. The FDD includes a list of existing and former franchisees – use that list; it's one of the most important tools for franchise exploration.

Existing franchisees will talk to you by phone, or if they're in close proximity to you, they may invite you for a personal meeting. Some franchisees may not be willing to talk to you at all, but most franchisees remember what it was like when they were exploring franchise opportunities, and they're willing to help you because someone once helped them. Franchisees also realize that it's important for their franchise networks to expand – it gives them greater visibility in the marketplace (more franchisees means more money in the national advertising fund) and greater clout when negotiating with suppliers.

Here's an idea that you will find extremely helpful: Go to work for an existing franchisee. Offer to work weekends or part time for a month or more to experience the franchise operation. This is a practical way for you to discover your interest in a specific business. Many franchisors will require that you at least meet with an existing franchisee to discuss your prospects for joining the franchise network.

"Are franchisees getting paid to tell me good things so that I'll buy the franchise?" If they are, the information will be revealed in the FDD, or the franchisor is violating federal laws in the U.S.! Generally, franchisors do not pay franchisees for speaking to prospective franchisees. However, franchisors sometimes sponsor competitions (i.e. the franchisee who helps sell the most franchises in a year receives $10,000!). But that information also must be disclosed in the FDD.

Questions you should ask:

- *Would you buy this same franchise again?*
- *What are the franchisor's greatest strengths . . . weaknesses?*
- *How much money can I expect to earn after a year as a franchisee? After three years?*

14. Decide if You Can Afford the Investment

Study Item 7 of the franchisor's FDD to understand your financial commitment when you buy this franchise. Federal law requires U.S. franchisors to clearly disclose financial information in the FDD. Item 7, Estimated Initial Investment, presents each financial commitment in a chart that shows you when the money is due to be paid, to whom it must be paid (i.e. the franchisor, a media company, a landlord, or a supplier), and whether or not the money is refundable. This is the best way to see the required financial commitment at a glance.

Keep in mind that the franchisor must include every financial requirement in Item 7, which eliminates surprises.

"Oh, we didn't tell you that you owe $5,000 for training?" That sort of thing doesn't happen anymore in franchising.

Questions you should ask:

- *Can I afford to invest this amount of money?*
- *Do existing franchisees say that the investment is reasonable?*
- *How does this financial commitment compare to investments in competitive opportunities?*

15. Understand the Ongoing Fees

Look at the ongoing royalty and advertising fee requirements, which are not part of Item 7. Most franchisors require franchisees to pay a percentage of gross sales as a royalty every month – the percentage may be as low as 5 percent and as high as 12 percent, and varies from company to company. The advertising fee is also a percentage of gross sales and may be in the range of 1 percent to 3 percent paid monthly.

Questions you should ask:

- *Do the royalty and advertising fees seem reasonable?*
- *How does the franchisor spend the royalty dollars paid by franchisees?*
- *Is the national advertising fund effective for boosting retail sales?*

16. Get Help!

Consult with your professional advisors. You should spend the money to engage a franchise attorney and an accountant prior to signing a franchise agreement. There are many franchise attorneys at work in the U.S. and other countries. You can find them through a franchise association such as the International Franchise Association (franchise.org). You will likely pay $500 to $1,500 for the attorney's basic services. You will likely pay more money to an attorney who does not specialize in franchise law – that's like asking your franchise attorney to handle a personal injury suit. If an attorney suggests he/she negotiate with the franchisor on your behalf, be very careful. Franchisors rarely negotiate and franchise attorneys know that. However, franchise attorneys also know areas in which a franchisor is likely to negotiate and may be helpful in that regard.

It's more difficult to find an accountant who is familiar with franchising and who understands franchising. Too often accountants are anti-franchising and they advise their clients to start businesses independently rather than to join a franchise network and pay fees. That's unfortunate because statistics demonstrate that in many industries franchises are more successful than independently owned businesses. My best advice for finding a "franchise friendly" accountant is to find an accountant who is also a franchisee! In other words, the accountant's practice is part of a franchise network. You can find these businesses through franchise associations. A good accountant will be able to help you develop a business plan and assess your financial risk as well as rewards. Accounting fees vary widely, but for basic services expect to pay $500 to $1,500. Keep in mind that you also may need an accountant after you become a franchisee to prepare your quarterly and annual statements.

Keep in mind that professional advisors are not supposed to make decisions for you. "Should I buy this franchise?" is a question that a good advisor will not answer. Advisors will point out pros and cons; ultimately, you make the decisions.

Other possible advisors include franchise brokers and coaches. When you engage these advisors, make certain that you understand what's in it for them. Brokers sell franchises for a living; they do not advise franchise prospects except as part of their mission to sell a franchise. Brokers generally do not charge fees to their clients because the franchisor pays them when they sell a franchise. There's nothing wrong with this arrangement, by the way, and franchisors who rely on brokers must reveal this information in the FDD.

Questions you should ask:

- *How does this franchise opportunity compare to others you've reviewed?*
- *What are the problem areas that you see investing in this type of franchise?*
- *Based on my financial situation, is this a franchise I can afford?*

17. Make Your Final Decision

Take a deep breath, offer up any final prayers, and say yes to the franchisor of your choice. Go ahead; sign the franchise agreement. Congratulations, you're a franchisee! If you did your homework, and followed the recommendations offered to you in this book and through other sources, you're on your way to stardom!

Questions you should ask:

- *When does my training session begin?*
- *What three things must I be sure to do to succeed in this business?*
- *What three things must I be sure* not *to do to succeed in this business?*

When I'm buying a franchise, and when I coach my clients who are buying franchises, I use these 17 steps to success. Each step includes multiple tasks, and it's important to take the time to complete each step. If you have questions about how to complete these steps, or you need additional guidance, visit my blog at HowToBuyAFranchise.com and contact me.

FUNDING YOUR FRANCHISE ACQUISITION: WHERE DO YOU GET THE MONEY?

Two common mistakes that prospective franchisees make when they're exploring franchise opportunities are (1) ignorance of their personal financial status and capabilities; and (2) ignorance of the financial requirements to buy a franchise.

Do you know your credit score and how much cash you can invest in a franchise or bring to the table to leverage additional funds? Do you know what banks, leasing companies, the U.S Small Business Administration, and special funds designated for franchise lending will require of you to secure a loan?

The sooner you get on top of these issues the better – otherwise, you may be wasting your time. You should expect franchisors and franchise brokers to ask you these questions even before they give you a Franchise Disclosure Document. Not to do so could mean the franchisor is wasting time because you may not be financially qualified to acquire the franchise.

Good News for Borrowers

If you need to borrow money to acquire a franchise, the good news is that for the first time in many years you have multiple options available. While it was nearly impossible to borrow money to start a franchise between 2008 and 2010, opportunities are more plentiful today but still not what they were before the Great Recession.

While there's still not a national lender for franchise opportunities as existed prior to 2008, nowadays more community banks lend to franchisees, more franchisors lend to franchisees, several franchise-specific funds underwrite franchise acquisitions, and for those who have a retirement fund, the fund can be rolled into seed money to capitalize a business.

"Compared to what it was like before the recession, funding franchises is still difficult," explains Bob Coleman, editor of the Coleman Report, which provides information to bankers to help them make less risky small-business loans. "Lenders are scrutinizing deals and are particularly interested in the performance of the brand, something that didn't matter as much previously."

Not Good News for New Brands

"Unless a franchisor has 80 to 100 units, there's no deal," continues Coleman. "A startup brand and a new franchisee is not a favorable combination. Lenders want to see track records by both the brand and the franchisee. Lenders today know about unhappy franchisees and how to check for them, whereas (previously) they didn't care – [pay] 30 percent [money] down and you'd get the loan, but that doesn't happen anymore."

According to Coleman, lenders view franchises as "a little bit better risk than mom-and-pop businesses," but they're insisting on funding deals for established brands. They also prefer experienced franchisees. "If you've been successfully operating a unit for several years and now you need money to open another one to three units, you can get that money."

Franchising is Growing Once Again

As the economy continues to grow, lenders are becoming more receptive to franchise deals, and franchise companies are growing, too. In fact, Frandata, the franchise information firm based outside of Washington, D.C., reported that franchising is now growing at its fastest rate in five years, largely because prospective and existing franchisees have been able to find money to buy franchises.

How Do You Get a Loan Today?

So what's it going to take today to get the money you need to acquire a franchise opportunity?

Business financing expert Doug Smith of Biz Finance Solutions (bizfinancesolutions.com) in Colorado, explains that there are two types of funding: equity-based and debt-based.

"Using the money you have in your retirement plan, rolling it over without penalty or taxation, and using it as an injection to get a U.S. government-backed loan is equity financing," he says, and it's an option that many franchisees use today.

"Debt based funding requires a credit score and credit history to get a conventional bank loan or unsecured business financing, including equipment leasing, and unsecured personal loans. But if your credit score is weak or you've filed a bankruptcy, it's the kiss of death."

Your personal financial situation, and your thoughts about financial risk, may determine how you should proceed when you seek financing.

The 401(k) Rollover

Smith's preferred franchise funding strategy is the 401(k) Rollover, and most people don't seem to know about it. Or if they do, they've been told it's illegal or dangerous. However, this option has the blessing of the U.S. government.

Here are the facts you need to know:

If you have a retirement fund and you change employers, you have three important options:

1. Leave the fund where it is. The majority of people choose this option.

2. Move the fund into a new account, such as a self-directed IRA.

3. Move the fund to your new employer's 401(k), thus consolidating your retirement savings in one fund.

Most people aren't aware of Option #3, beginning with becoming your own employer!

That is, you can become a franchisee and establish a C Corporation with stock and a 401(k). Becoming your own employer puts you in the enviable position of self-funding your own business, tax-free! You can move – or what the Internal Revenue Service refers to as rollover – your existing retirement money into your new employer's 401k, and the cash can be used to buy and operate a franchise. It's tax-free, penalty-free (if done correctly), and it's legal. It may be your best option for funding your business, particularly if you don't have other resources, or you can't qualify for a traditional loan.

Isn't This Controversial?

The U.S. Internal Revenue Service and the Department of Labor have established guidelines and directives for implementing a 401(k) Rollover. You can't use the rollover to dodge taxes or to personally benefit from the money. Some years ago a financial broker was shut down for a period of time for stretching the rules, and that incident gave rise to the notion that the rollover is illegal. It's not. If you use the rollover for the right reasons – you can't use it for a scheme; it has to be used with a real business – you (or your advisor) set it up correctly and comply annually with the regulations, you should be able to avoid any objections or complications. Follow the spirit of the guidelines with appropriate intentions and you should remain in the clear.

Of course, the IRS reserves the right to change the rules, and that's why it's extremely important that you work with a credible company or broker that has a track record for successfully implementing and maintaining rollovers.

Two Benefits of a 401(k) Rollover

The 401(k) Rollover has made a good name for itself among franchisors, who frequently recommend the strategy to prospective franchisees.

Here are two reasons why:

If the franchise acquisition is a small investment – under $150,000 – franchisors know that lenders aren't attracted to small loans. There's no money to be made processing small loans, so lenders avoid them. That makes a rollover more attractive. Rollover money can be used to pay for the franchise fee and to buy equipment. When you don't have collateral – or you're buying a business that provides a service from your home, a vehicle, or a small office – the 401(k) Rollover may be your best choice for funding your business.

After a rollover, you can use the cash as equity to qualify for a conventional or SBA-guaranteed loan. You'll likely need a cash injection of 30 percent to secure a loan. In the past, borrowers used equity in real estate (i.e. their personal residence) to qualify for a loan. Now you can use rollover money for your cash injection.

"People who utilize a rollover are more successful in the average business," reveals Geoff Seiber, president and CEO of FranFund (franfund.com) in Fort Worth, Texas. "People who use this strategy tend to stay in business longer because they used their retirement money to fund their business and they don't have debt to service."

Can You Accept the Risks?

Used properly, the 401(k) Rollover is an aggressive way to capitalize your business. The challenge, however, is that by using it you give up the security of a retirement fund. Some people can't handle that emotionally. *Can you?* Will you feel comfortable knowing that your retirement money is now invested in your own business? If not, you probably don't want to use this funding strategy. On the other hand, people who start businesses and plan to operate them aren't usually looking for comfort.

In the U.S., numerous companies provide rollover services, including: Biz Finance Solutions, Guidant, FranFund, and Benetrends. Expect to spend about $5,000 with one of these firms to set up your rollover. The firm will also offer to provide necessary administrative services to keep your fund in check, and that may cost you about $100 monthly.

It's important to keep your rollover plan in compliance with the laws because the IRS audits these plans. "Under 2 percent of our plans are audited every year," says Seiber, "which is the norm in our industry. By not doing the administrative work properly, you're taking a bigger risk" if the IRS audits your account.

Unless you have a pile of cash that you intend to inject into your deal (i.e. a retirement fund that you will rollover or savings that you will bring to the table), your funding options are severely limited. It's even worse if you're a new franchisee and you want to buy a single unit – an existing franchisee with plans to expand or a multi-unit operator will find more options.

Look to Your Franchisor for Funding

Guys like Coleman, Smith, and Seiber are among a select corps of experts who can advise prospective franchisees when they need financing, but there's only so much they can do in a reticent financial market. If you can't take advantage of the programs they offer or recommend, your best source of funding may be your franchisor of choice. If you know that you will need money to acquire a franchise, look for franchisors who lend to franchisees. Even franchisors who don't loan money to franchisees know who will (and what's required), so ask your finance-related questions early in your franchise exploration.

And don't give up! Some of the most successful franchisees today started out by investing in a low-cost franchise and expanding when they could afford to do so. Many others started out with money borrowed from family and friends. If franchising makes sense for you, you'll find a franchise company that will help you clear the lending hurdles.

Here's One More Funding Option: VetFran

VetFran®, sponsored by the International Franchise Association (IFA) (www.franchise.org), helps veterans of the U.S. armed services buy franchise opportunities by providing financial assistance, training, and industry support.

VetFran was created by the late Don Dwyer Sr. –founder of The Dwyer Group, a conglomerate of franchise companies, to say "thank you" to America's veterans returning from the first Gulf War. After the Sept. 11, 2001 terrorist attacks, IFA re-launched VetFran and the program continues to this day.

Nearly 650 franchise brands voluntarily offer financial incentives and mentoring to prospective franchisees who are veterans. Thousands of veterans have utilized VetFran to buy franchises. If you're a veteran, be sure to ask your franchisor of choice, "Do you support VetFran?" This may be an additional source of funding for you.

FOREIGN INVESTORS: USE FRANCHISING TO GET A U.S. GREEN CARD

Foreign investors who want to move to the USA are taking advantage of the Immigrant Investor Program administered by the U.S. Citizenship and Immigration Services (USCIS). Applications are rising rapidly due to favorable changes in the program, and in part due to franchising.

Known as EB-5, the program was created to stimulate the U.S. economy through job creation and capital investment.

Here's how it works:

How the EB5 program works

A qualified foreigner invests $1-million directly into a business or into a regional fund that invests in businesses, including franchises of all types. If the investment creates at least 10 full-time jobs for at least two years, the investor gets a green card and eventually U.S. citizenship. In high unemployment areas, and rural areas, the investment is $500,000.

Foreign investors are using EB-5 to move their families to the U.S. or to send their children to the U.S. to study. A married investor gets visas for himself, his spouse, and all unmarried children under the age of 21.

Franchisors favor foreign operators

Foreigners operate many franchised businesses in the U.S. and franchisors welcome them because they are enthusiastic about learning a successful operating system that they and their family members can operate. However, EB-5 does not require investors to actually work in a business. As long as they fulfill the requirements of EB-5, the investors can live wherever they choose, start their own business, take a job, or retire in the U.S.!

As with any bureaucratic program, EB-5 takes time to complete. Investors must prove their money came from a lawful source and must also pass the scrutiny of U.S. immigration investors. The entire process may require a year before the investor and family can move to the U.S.

Direct and in-direct jobs count

Until recently, most EB-5 investors preferred real estate projects, but many of those investments failed to meet the job requirements. Franchising, on the other hand, is a much better choice. An injection of $1-million invested into certain franchised businesses can create upwards of 40 jobs. Consider, for example, a convenience store franchise. The franchise itself may need only 4 to 6 employees, but indirect jobs also count. A convenience store sells food and beverages and indirectly creates jobs to provide those products. Those indirect jobs count.

Franchisors are unaware of EB-5

Many franchise networks include multi-unit operators who seek expansion capital, and sometimes partners, to open a dozen or more units, or to expand into a new territory.

However, most franchisors don't know this program exists, so their multi-unit operators may not know, either.

The USCIS.com is a good place to learn more about this program.

FRANCHISE TERMS AND RESOURCES

The following lists provide information about franchising, including resources that may help you while you're pursuing a franchise opportunity. Please keep in mind that the inclusion of any resource does not imply the author's endorsement. The information in these lists is not exhaustive. If you're looking for something that you can't find in this section, please visit HowToBuyAFranchise.com and use our Contact form.

Franchise Terms

Here are some of the most common terms used in franchising.

Advertising Fee

Many franchise opportunities require franchisees to pay a monthly fee into an Advertising or Marketing Fund. The fee is generally represented as a percentage (for example, 2 percent) and is almost always calculated on the franchisee's gross sales, as opposed to net sales or profits. The Advertising Fee may also be a flat fee. The Advertising Fee is ongoing and will be collected while the franchise agreement is in effect. Advertising Fund monies are used to advertise the franchise brand, its products and/or services. This is not money to be used by the franchisor!

Ad Fund

Franchisees pay their Advertising Fees into an Ad Fund, which is used to underwrite the cost of advertising and promotions for franchisees. The franchisor, or Franchise Advisory Council, establishes the Ad Fund and oversees it on behalf of franchisees. Ad Fund money is often used to hire advertising and marketing agencies to assist the franchise network.

Disclosure

In some countries, and especially in the United States, franchisors are *required* by federal and some state laws to "disclose" individuals who are serious about acquiring a franchise. Disclosure is a process that includes providing prospective franchisees with a copy of the franchisor's Franchise Disclosure Document (FDD) and Franchise Agreement. The FDD must be delivered to a franchise candidate at least 14 days prior to the candidate purchasing the franchise. Disclosure minimizes fraudulent sales in franchising and promotes the safety and longevity of franchising. Franchisors are required to comply with specific disclosure regulations that disseminate helpful information to prospective franchisees in advance of paying any money or signing any documents.

Disclosure Document

See Franchise Disclosure Document.

Earning's Claim

An Earning's Claim (or a Financial Performance Representation) may be included in a franchisor's Franchise

Disclosure Document. An Earning's Claim documents the earnings of franchisees in the franchisor's network. *Most franchisors do not include Earning's Claims in their documents.* Those who do not are prohibited from making any oral or written statements concerning the actual or potential sales, costs, income or profits of their franchise opportunities.

Franchise

It's a license that grants an individual or an entity (i.e. a corporation) the right to use a franchisor's operating system for the purpose of marketing, selling and distributing the franchisor's products and/or services. A franchise is a license.

Franchise Agreement

A legal document (license) signed by both the franchisor and the franchisee granting the franchisee the right to operate the franchise system for a specified period of time, in a specified format, and sometimes in a specified location. It's the legally binding document between franchisor and franchisee.

Franchise Associations

There are approximately 40 trade associations throughout the world that represent the interests of franchisors and franchisees. See International Franchise Association.

Franchise Disclosure Document

Every franchisor in the United States is required to complete and maintain a Franchise Disclosure Document (FDD). The FDD, in layperson's language, describes the franchise opportunity. The items of disclosure are standard for all franchise companies. There are 23 Items that require disclosure, including Litigation, Initial Franchise Fee, Franchisee's Obligations, Franchisor's Obligations, Territory, Restrictions On What The Franchisee May Sell, Renewal, Termination, Transfer and Dispute Resolution, List of Outlets (Franchisees), Financial Statements, and more. Prospective franchisees should read the FDD several times before investing in the franchise.

Franchisee

The individual or entity (i.e. a corporation) that's assigned the rights to a franchise by a franchisor.

Franchise Expo

Franchise companies come together under one roof to exhibit their franchise opportunities for a day or more. The public is invited to these events. Expos sometimes include educational programs.

Franchise Fee

A one-time, upfront fee required by the franchisor. It must be disclosed in the Franchise Disclosure Document.

Franchise Portal

A website that promotes franchise opportunities and may also include educational information about franchising. The best example: FranchiseExpo.com.

Franchisor

The company that grants franchises to franchisees. The franchisor controls and owns the franchise system.

International Franchise Association

IFA is the world's largest trade organization representing both franchisors and franchisees. Headquarters: Washington, D.C. Website: franchise.org.

International Franchise Expo

The world's premier event among franchise expos is sponsored by the International Franchise Association. The producer of the IFE is MFVExpositions. Website: ifeinfo.com.

Royalty Fee

A payment of money by the franchisee to the franchisor. Usually represented as a percentage (as an example, 6 percent) and paid weekly or monthly. May also be a flat weekly or monthly fee. Royalties are almost always paid on the franchisee's gross sales, as opposed to net sales or profits. This is an ongoing fee that must be paid during the period of time the franchise agreement/license is in effect. The royalty fee must be disclosed in the Franchise Disclosure Document.

FRANCHISE RESOURCES

FRANCHISE ASSOCIATIONS

International Franchise Association

1900 K St., NW, Suite 700
Washington, DC 20006
Phone: (202) 628-8000
Website: franchise.org

In addition to representing franchisors and franchisees, the IFA also represents the Council of Franchise Suppliers, which includes attorneys, accountants, consultants, franchise brokers, and others who may be able to assist you in your exploration of franchising. IFA promotes numerous books and other resources about franchising and publishes *Franchising World* magazine. Free resources are included on the IFA's website.

Canadian Franchise Association

5399 Eglinton Ave. West, Suite 116
Toronto, Ontario
Canada M9C 5K6
Telephone: 416-695-2896
Email: info@cfa.ca

Website: cfa.ca

For a list of Franchise Associations Worldwide:
www.franchise.org

FRANCHISE EXPOSITIONS

MFV Expositions

Telephone: 201-226-1130
Website: mfvexpo.com

In addition to the International Franchise Expo, MFV Expositions produces the West Coast Franchise Expo, Franchise Expo South and international franchise events including *Feria Internacional de Franquicias* in Mexico City.

U.S. GOVERNMENT RESOURCES

U.S. Small Business Administration: www.sba.gov

U.S. Commerce Department International Trade Administration: ita.doc.gov

BOOKS, PERIODICALS & PORTALS

7 Dirty Little Secrets of Franchising: Protect Your Franchise Investment, Amazon.com
12 Amazing Franchise Opportunities for 2015, Amazon.com
101 Questions to Ask Before You Invest in a Franchise, Amazon.com
Bond's Franchise Guide, Amazon.com
Buy "Hot" Franchises Without Getting Burned, Amazon.com
Entrepreneur, entrepreneur.com, publishes the Franchise 500 every January
Franchise Handbook, franchisehandbook.com
FranchiseExpo.com franchiseexpo.com
FranchiseGator.com franchisegator.com
Franchise Opportunities Guide, franchise.org
Franchise Times, franchisetimes.com
Franchise Update, franchise-update.com
Franchising World, franchise.org

AUTHOR'S BIOGRAPHY

John P. Hayes, Ph.D., began working in the franchise community in 1979 as a freelance writer. He continues to write about franchising for media worldwide, including newspapers, magazines and books. On several occasions he has been a franchisee, and for several years he served as the President & CEO of one of America's major franchise companies, HomeVestors of America, Inc. He is one of the few people to have been a franchisee, a franchisor, and an advisor to franchisors and franchisees.

For many years John's client list included the International Franchise Association (IFA), the International Franchise Expo (IFE), and dozens of franchise companies. For several years he toured the U.S. as a part of IFA's regional training faculty, and on many occasions he has been a speaker and trainer for IFA, the IFE, and countless franchise companies. For several years starting in 1989, he traveled with the IFA's international franchise trade missions, marketing U.S. franchise opportunities in Europe, South America, the Pacific Rim, and the Far East.

John is a frequent speaker at international franchise expos and a guest on radio and television to discuss franchise topics. He was featured in a 30-minute television infomercial called *The Power of Franchising*. Through the years he has assisted franchisors and franchisees internationally to sell or acquire master licensing rights. For nearly 30 years he has taught the most popular symposium at the International Franchise Expo: The A to Zs of Buying a Franchise.

He is the co-author of *Franchising: The Inside Story* (with franchisor John Kinch); *You Can't Teach a Kid to Ride a Bike at a Seminar* (with franchisor David Sandler); *Start Small, Finish Big, 15 Lessons to Start & Operate Your Own Business* (with the co-founder of Subway); and *Network Marketing for Dummies* (with Zig Ziglar).

Your Personal Franchise Coach:
Dr. John P. Hayes

Schedule private, one-on-one coaching sessions with franchise and business-building expert, Dr. John Hayes. See www.howtobuyafranchise.com.

Coaching especially for:

Prospective Franchisees

Existing Franchisees

Startup Franchisors

Startup businesses

Partnerships

Family Businesses

Network Marketers

You select the topics to discuss, including:

Buying a franchise; becoming a franchisee

Are you the right fit for becoming a franchisor or franchisee?

Capturing and keeping the right customers in your business

How to sell franchises (domestically, internationally)

Developing a Franchise Advisory Council

Marketing Master Licenses internationally

Building your Leadership Team to manage your business

Working "on" your business and not always "in" your business

Developing training and support systems for your franchisees

Improving the franchisor/franchisee relationship

Creating an Ops program that benefits franchisor and franchisees

Writing a book to promote your business

Other topics of your choice

Message to Prospective Franchisees:

I do not sell franchises and I am not a broker for any franchise concept. First and foremost, I will help you determine if franchising makes sense for you. If it doesn't, save your time, save your money, and move on.

If franchising makes sense for you, I'll help you explore the type of franchise that would be best suited to your interests, skills, values and economic situation. As you conduct your due diligence (in part by asking/answering the questions in *101 Questions to Ask Before You Invest in a Franchise*), I'll look over your shoulder and guide you along the way. You can rely on me to help you walk through the minefield of franchise discovery. Along the way I'll introduce you to professionals (i.e. accountants, attorneys, brokers, advisors) who can assist you as you acquire a franchise.

Choose One Session or Multiple Sessions

Whether you need just one session or you want to schedule weekly sessions, the choice is yours.

Discounts are available for more than three sessions. You may include partners or other members of your corporate team on the same coaching call for one fee. Details available at howtobuyafranchise.com.

BizCom Press

Do you have a story to tell that will help others improve their life, their business, or otherwise make a difference? BizComPress can help you reach the widest audience possible. Founded by authors for authors, BizComPress is a new kind of publishing company. Our award-winning team will help you write your book, edit it, design it, publish it, and promote it. And you keep the majority of your earnings!

Whether you already have a manuscript, or just the seed of an idea, contact us and we'll provide honest feedback based on decades of experience in book publishing. If we think the manuscript or the idea has a market, we can develop a plan that fits your budget. You'll be on your way to becoming a published author.

For more information contact Scott White at 214-458-5751 or contact Scott via BizComPress.

Your Opinion Is Valuable to Me!

When you've finished reading this book, please take a few moments and post a review at Amazon.com. I'd appreciate hearing from you, and I value your opinions. Plus, the best way to sell a book is by a review – so I'm asking you to please help others discover this book with a review that you post. It takes only a few moments to write a line or two about the book and then post it on Amazon.com. Thank you in advance!

Discover other books by Dr. John P. Hayes
Visit: BooksbyJohnHayes.com

CPSIA information can be obtained
at www.ICGtesting.com
Printed in the USA
LVOW13s2311060717
540524LV00008B/115/P